ASSESSMENT AND DOCUMENTATION IN EARLY CHILDHOOD EDUCATION

Documentation in early childhood education is typically seen as a means to enhance the quality of care and education, and as a way to take account of the child's view.

Assessment and Documentation in Early Childhood Education considers the increasing trend towards systematic child documentation especially in early childhood institutions. The authors present ways in which assessment and evaluation are done sometimes explicitly but more often implicitly in these practices, and explore their means, aims, forms and functions. They also examine the rationalities of child documentation from the perspective of professional practice and professionalism, and suggest that documentation and assessment practices can weaken and constrain but also empower and strengthen teachers, children and parents. Topics explored include:

- different forms of documentation and assessment;
- documentation and listening to the children;
- dilemmas of assessment and documentation;
- participation by children;
- involvement of parents.

This timely book will appeal to those studying in the fields of early childhood education, teacher education, special education, general education, social work, counselling, psychology, sociology, childhood studies and family studies.

Maarit Alasuutari is Professor of Social Work (FT) at the University of Jyväskylä, Finland.

Ann-Marie Markström is Associate Professor in Education at Linköping University, Sweden.

Ann-Christine Vallberg-Roth is Professor of Early Childhood Education in the Centre for Profession Studies (CPS) at the University of Malmö, Sweden.

ASSESSMENT AND DOCUMENTATION IN EARLY CHILDHOOD EDUCATION

*Maarit Alasuutari, Ann-Marie Markström
and Ann-Christine Vallberg-Roth*

Routledge
Taylor & Francis Group

LONDON AND NEW YORK

First published 2014
by Routledge
2 Park Square, Milton Park, Abingdon, Oxon OX14 4RN

and by Routledge
711 Third Avenue, New York, NY 10017

Routledge is an imprint of the Taylor & Francis Group, an informa business

British Library Cataloguing in Publication Data
A catalogue record for this book is available from the British Library

Library of Congress Cataloging in Publication Data
Alasuutari, Maarit.
Assessment and documentation in early childhood education / Maarit
Alasuutari, Ann-Marie Markström, Ann-Christine Vallberg-Roth.
pages cm
1. Early childhood education—Scandinavia. 2. Educational evaluation—
Scandinavia. I. Markström, Ann-Marie. II. Vallberg-Roth, Ann-Christine. III.
Title.
LB1139.3.S34A43 2014
372.210948—dc23
2013030920

ISBN: 978-0-415-66125-6 (hbk)
ISBN: 978-0-415-66126-3 (pbk)
ISBN: 978-1-315-81850-4 (ebk)

Typeset in Bembo
by Book Now Ltd, London

CONTENTS

ACKNOWLEDGEMENTS

This book links and combines the work of three scholars from Finland and Sweden. There are several people and organizations that have supported us in our work. We are grateful to Professor emerita Gunilla Halldén from the University of Linköping for her support and for giving a start to the collaboration by introducing Maarit and Ann-Marie to each other. A little later, the duo grew into a trio when all three of us got to know each other and Ann-Christine joined the group.

We also thank our colleagues at the Universities of Jyväskylä, Linköping, Malmö and Tampere. A particular debt is owed to Associate Professor Maria Simonsson at the University of Linköping, and to Professor Sven Persson and Professor Ingegerd Tallberg Broman and her project 'Childhood in multiple contexts' at the University of Malmö. The research that this book is based on has been funded by the following organizations: the Faculty of Education (University of Linköping); Centre for Profession Studies (CPS) (University of Malmö); the Centre for Advanced Study (University of Tampere); Academy of Finland; The Swedish Research Council; and Ministry of Education and Research in Norway. Furthermore, the grant of The Finnish Association of Non-fiction Writers has helped us in covering the travel costs of our collaboration.

Additionally, we are grateful to Damian Finnegan, Sue Glover Frykman, Matt Goodman, Peter Holley, Sean Kearns and Maiju Virkajärvi who have polished our English. A final note of thanks to our families who have taken turns in hosting our intensive and talkative writing seminars. Thank you for your support and patience.

Maarit Alasuutari   Ann-Marie Markström   Ann-Christine Vallberg-Roth

1

INTRODUCTION

The following story presents an everyday example of the whole of the documentation concerning an individual child in contemporary early childhood education (ECE).

> First, the parents fill in an application, consisting of inquiries about the child and the family, to get their child admitted to ECE. Before the child starts her or his early education, the teacher pays a visit to the home to get to know the child and the family, and to learn about the parents' expectations. The teacher uses a locally designed form to structure the discussion and to document it. After the child has started her or his ECE, the teacher and the parent(s) jointly draft an individual educational plan (IEP) for the child on a specific form. The child might be involved in this for a short period. The plan is then followed once or twice a year by using the same form. Additionally, the child's learning, interests and activities are documented in a portfolio. The portfolio is introduced to the parents and they are also encouraged to record their observations in it. Moreover, it is increasingly common that the staff maintain contact with the parents via e-mail. E-mail is used to inform the parents about the activities arranged by the institution and to report to them regarding the behaviour and progress of their child. Additionally, the staff builds a portfolio of the activities of the whole child group, either as hard copy or in digital form. The practitioners also register the number of hours per day that the child attends ECE in a computerized system. If the child moves to another group of children, a meeting is held between the family and the staff members of the old and the new groups. This meeting is also documented. Finally, specific screening methods are used to assess the child's development and school readiness at specific ages.

The above story is composed from an interview with an ECE official in a Finnish town. It depicts the documentation practices that are routinely used with every child in the local ECE centres. Even though the story is from a specific context, it exemplifies a more general trend in early childhood education: various documentation and registering practices have become an integral part of its daily life (cf. Jensen, Broström & Hansen, 2010).

The story also reveals that child documentation seems to serve different functions in ECE and it is only rarely explicitly linked with the other main topic in this book: child assessment. In the story, the tools that are used to examine the child's development at specific ages are the only documentation that is talked about as assessment. Otherwise, the documentation seems to have other functions. Some documentation is used mainly for the sake of administration, like the application form and the registration of the hours during which the child attends ECE. More often, documentation seems to deal with the particular early education centre and the specific group of children. As seen in the above example, it is used to record and provide information on their activities through the creation of a group portfolio and via e-mail exchanges with parents. Documentation is also important in evaluating and planning the educational work and other activities of the institution and in showing accountability. Finally, child documentation is done for the sake of individual children and families. It is used to support the children's development and learning, and their participation in ECE, as well as parental involvement in early education. These more generic motivations for child documentation derive usually from the aims to enhance the quality of ECE, both through its pedagogical work and through collaboration with parents (see OECD, 2006). Additionally, child documentation can be seen as a means to provide individualized and child-centred early education (Carr & Lee, 2012; Driscoll & Rudge, 2005).

In this book we are interested in the child documentation, the impetus of which is connected to the pedagogical work of ECE, to the learning, development and participation of children, and to collaboration with parents. We discuss practices such as pedagogical documentation, learning stories, individual educational and developmental plans (IEPs and IDPs), portfolios, and standardized measures, along with forms and questionnaires aimed at parents and children. Often these documentation tools are labelled and seen as something other than assessment. However, we argue that much of the child documentation that takes place on a regular basis in ECE is intertwined with assessment, even though this may not be its primary aim. Hence, we do not take the specific theoretical backgrounds of different documentation practices as our starting points but adopt a more critical stance. We consider, on the one hand, how children are assessed and documented and, on the other hand, how they are documented and assessed though different documentation practices in ECE. We also take into account children's participation in documentation and the involvement of parents. Consequently, we discuss child documentation as a boundary object regarding the teacher, parent and the child (or regarding the institution and the home). Drawing on our studies in the Nordic context, we analyse and give examples of what forms of documentation are used in ECE and how documentation is deployed in practice. We also study the functions of documentation and how it governs the gaze on children and childhood as well as on parents, parenthood and professionals, and on ECE as an institution in contemporary society. We do not present ideas or models of 'good' documentation, but we hope to participate in the development of ECE by providing a thought-provoking discussion on assessment and documentation and their dilemmas.

Assessment in the Nordic ECE

Historically, documenting and observing children in ECE is not new. For example, Lenz-Taguchi (2000) argues that child observation and documentation have been conducted in Swedish early education throughout the twentieth century for various purposes, starting from medically-focused forms of documentation in the early twentieth century, developing later into psychologically-oriented observation and documentation. She notes that the decentralization of the steering system of ECE services – a phenomenon that is recognizable in different forms from the 1980s onwards in the welfare services of many countries – led to an increased interest in observation and documentation in the 1990s.

However, documentation is not usually associated with assessment in Nordic ECE – something that was also exemplified in the story in the beginning of this chapter. Overall, assessment is a culturally contradictory issue in Nordic ECE. Traditionally, the whole of the child's care, education and instruction – 'educare thinking' – has been at the core of the ECE ideologies, along with the child's social development, play and peer relations. Formal lessons and learning are seen as the domain of compulsory education (Lidholt, 2001; Niikko, 2006; Wagner, 2006). For instance, Finnish preschool – that is, early education provided for all six-year-olds during the year preceding compulsory education – does not aim to teach children to read. Instead, learning to read and write is defined as the goal of the first grade at school. Formal lessons and school-type education are not understood as belonging to a good childhood. This aligns with the thinking in other Nordic countries too (Wagner, 2006). As a result, assessment is usually not regarded as a part of ECE. Even though documentation can be underlined in the institutions (e.g. Lpfö98, 2010) and explicit assessment tools seem to be more common, assessment as an activity and task is still seen mainly as something that early educators in the Nordic ECE do not engage in, but rather something that the children will encounter when in school.

Furthermore, it seems that what is meant by assessment is ambiguous. In present-day literature, it may mean to evaluate or analyse something, to estimate, to give a review, assess or rate someone or something (Vallberg-Roth, 2012b). Sometimes assessment is used as a synonym for, or mixed with, the concept of evaluation. In this book we differentiate between these two concepts. We apply assessment when discussing an examination focusing on the individual, group or activity level. By evaluation we refer to an analysis at the institutional, system and programme level (cf. Sheridan, 2009). Considering the aims of the book, our discussion focuses mainly on assessment.

Our starting point is that assessment is, if not explicitly, implicitly part of ECE, and we will present examples about how it is intertwined in many of its ordinary documentation practices. Moreover, it is important to take into account that documentation and the assessment entangled with it does not only refer to written words, per se, but incorporates typically both written materials and talk (cf. Putnam & Cooren, 2004). Documentation can register assessments that are based on, or made in, talk and interaction. It can also be used as an invitation to assessment or to such talk that allows assessment in different social practices, for example, in parent–teacher discussions (Alasuutari & Markström, 2011; Markström, 2011a). These different practices of documentation and assessment are also illuminated in this book. Some chapters will consider assessment by studying mainly documentation – that is, written materials – but in some chapters the focus is on assessment as it is talked about or as it occurs in the intertwinement of written material and talk.

In this book we do not aim at promoting or suppressing any singular form of documentation or assessment, for example, on specific pedagogical grounds. Instead, we consider assessment and documentation from various perspectives that all entail a critical stance to the benevolent functions that they are primarily considered (only) to have. Principally, we draw on recent discussions on 'documentality' (Ferraris, 2013), but also the literature that considers the role and agency of documents and 'matter', or other objects in social life that have inspired us (e.g. Barad, 2007; Latour, 2005; Prior, 2003). Furthermore, the approach of governance (e.g. Miller & Rose, 2008; Rose, 1996b), which can be linked with documentality, provides an important starting point to some sections of the book.

'Documentality', documentation and agency

In social research as well as in contemporary life, documents are mainly seen as sources of evidence and receptacles of inert content. This implies an understanding of documents as (neutral) artefacts, exterior to the social interaction and its agents (Prior, 2003, 2008). Recently, this assumption has been challenged, especially, in the theory of 'documentality' and in literature drawing on Action Network Theory and post-humanist performativity. All these approaches provide bases for arguing for the agency of documents; even though they differ from each other, for example, in their notions of the human/subject and the nonhuman/object, as will be shown below.

'Documentality' is a concept introduced by Maurizio Ferraris (2013) and the name of his philosophical theory that presents a model of the social world. The basic argument of the theory is that social objects like money, marriages, childhood, students, education, bets, promises, assessments, the price of oil, taxes, parliaments and weekdays are the result of inscriptions or 'traces' of acts on some medium, for example on paper, in a computer file or in people's heads. Even though Ferraris takes a realistic stance to natural objects and sees them as existing in space and time independently of subjects, he argues that social objects are constructed, and that this is done specifically by inscription. According to him, 'there is nothing social outside the text' (ibid., p. 318). The text produces all that is social to us. However, the text needs to be understood broadly. It does not only refer to writing but also to communicating and using symbols more generally as well as to mental traces. Additionally, social objects always involve at least two persons.

Let's take an imaginary example from ECE. If a teacher, while observing a child, makes a mental note on some specific behaviour of the child, she produces an inscription. If the teacher never shares the mental note with anybody it cannot be called a social object in Ferraris' thinking. However, as soon as the teacher starts to discuss the observation with a colleague or any other person, or when she registers it on some medium, say, in the child's portfolio, a social object is constructed. Depending on the context, the object can be called, for example, a concern, an assessment, a problem child, a humorous story or information.

Hence, for the starting point of this book, Ferraris (2013) gives us the idea that not just face-to-face communication, but all kinds of registerings and documentations in ECE are essential in constructing the social world of the institution and the social objects of which this world comprises. Documentation is not something extra to the social life of ECE, but rather a fundamental part of it.

Ferraris (2013, pp. 247–96) also presents interesting arguments regarding institutions and documentation. He argues that institutions are specializations of social reality, and that they follow the same rules in their existence as social reality: institutional objects and institutions are constructed by documents. He also reserves the term 'document' only for inscriptions that have institutional value. Documents can be divided into two categories: weak and strong documents. Weak documents include merely the registration of facts (or issues). Strong documents, by contrast, are performatives. They are inscriptions of an act or an attestation that endures in time and has social value. For example, a university certificate changes a student to an MA, and this qualification stays with her. However, no document is weak or strong in itself but its character depends on the context. (The university certificate does not help if the student needs to prove her identity when entering a foreign country.) A strong document can become a weak one over time, and a weak document can be applied as a strong one in some context. For example, a memo of a child observation can be categorized as a weak document if it does not prescribe or cause any action. Nonetheless, if the memo is later used as evidence about the child's abilities and skills when assessing her development, for instance in a parent–teacher meeting, it turns into a strong document.

Ferraris (2013) distinguishes between subjects that have representations and objects that do not have them, but this division should not be understood as a foundational categorical difference. Instead, human beings are also social objects. Besides, while social objects depend on subjects – they would not exist if there were no subjects who could recognize them – they are not subjective. Ferraris also argues for privileging objects relative to subjects. According to him, 'what matters most are the objects that are in the world' (ibid., p. 13). Even though he does not use the notion of agency, his thinking implies that 'traces' and documentation have agency, since they perform and do things.

Another scholar who underlines the agency of documents is Lindsay Prior (2003, 2008). According to Prior, documents enter into systems of action as agents in their own right. They are not passive items but influence and structure the human agents as effectively as the agents influence the documents. In his thinking, Prior draws on Action Network Theory (ANT) that underlines the essential role and agency of objects in making human social life possible. The key theorist of ANT, Bruno Latour (2005, p. 71) states that '*any thing* that does modify a state of affairs by making a difference is an actor – or, if it has no figuration yet, an actant'. ANT applies the term nonhuman as an opposite of human and, in this way, tries to avoid excessively narrow implications for the words *object* and *thing*. It does not make specific arguments about the relative effects or power of humans and nonhumans, but defines them as 'participants in the course of action waiting to be given a figuration' (ibid.).

Françoir Cooren (2004) applies ANT in her examination of textual agency in organizations. She draws on the notion of 'hybrid agency', that is, 'the way humans can appropriate what nonhumans do' (Cooren, 2004, p. 377; c.f. Latour, 1994, 1996). Cooren (2004, p. 388) states that an organization can be seen as a hybrid of human and nonhuman contributions in which different documents display a form of agency by doing things that the humans alone could not do. Texts and documents 'participate in the channelling of behaviours, constitute and stabilize organizational pathways, and broadcast information/orders'. They can also create a semi-autonomous domain by referring to each other. Through a dense network of cross-referencing – that is, intertextuality – and shared textual formats, organizational documents can create a powerful version of social reality (Atkinson & Coffey, 2011, p. 90).

Let us consider the textual agency through a fictional example about an everyday textual practice in the Nordic ECE. Usually each child has a specific space in an ECE centre for her or his personal things, like back packs and spare cloths. Commonly, this space is identified with an individual tag. Through these tags – which present a form of a document – the educators produce order in the institution by directing the children to put their personal belongings in the right place. It does not take long after the presentation of the individual symbols until the educators become 'unnecessary': the children have learned their symbol and it directs their behaviour. The educators are not needed to guide and instruct the children on every occasion; the tags do it for them. This does not mean that human agency is considered to 'disappear' in relation to text. Instead, human appropriation is understood as always taking place, but the hybrid organization and the textual agency allow the humans (in this case the educators) to act from a distance (Cooren, 2004).

In its notion of hybrid agency, ANT exhibits similarities to post-humanist theorizing that considers the on-going performativity and 'intra-action' of material–discursive forms of agency (Barad, 2003, 2007). Hence, documentation is not a specific topic in the theorization; the approach discusses the relations of materiality and human life more generally. In comparison with ANT, post-humanist thinking seems to take a more extreme approach to the understanding of the human. It cuts loose from the traditional notions of human intentionality and subjectivity as the basis of agency.

Moreover, it calls into question the self-evidence of the differential categories of 'human' and 'nonhuman'. According to it, there are not pre-existing 'relata' or 'components' (like humans and documents) that interact. Instead, inseparability of these agentially intra-acting 'components' produces phenomena, within which differential exclusionary boundaries are marked. In the intra-acting, the discursive is constitutive of materiality, as the materiality is constitutive of the discursive; neither can be seen as the determinant of the other. Regarding documentation in ECE, the post-humanist approach calls us to consider the agentic character of different material tools, like official instructions, curricula, agendas and questionnaires, in creating phenomena that produce distinctions and delineate things for us. However, it also raises questions concerning how to relate to humans and human agency.

Hillevi Lenz-Taguchi (2010, 2012) applies a post-humanist approach in her discussion about the tool of pedagogical documentation in 'intra-active' pedagogy. She defines documentation as a material–discursive apparatus that is 'in itself' an active agent in generating discursive knowledge. Documentation is to be understood as 'matter/material', but not with a fixed essence. Instead, it can be seen as 'a substance in a process of intra-active performances and becoming' (2010, p. 61). In the intra-action it is impossible to draw a line between the subject or the knower and the object or known. Therefore, Lenz-Taguchi argues that, as educational practitioners, we are 'entangled with our observations and documentations – our apparatuses of knowing' (ibid., p. 69).

As was stated earlier, our starting point in this book is mainly informed by the work of Maurizio Ferraris (2013), although the ANT and post-humanist theorizing have also inspired our thinking. The agency of documentation and its essential role in constructing the social world are the key assumptions of our text. Even though we focus on the function of documentation in ECE, we also underline that documentation is a human enterprise. We consider documents in all their forms – visual, textual, digital, audio, etc. – as produced by humans and as appropriated by them.

Documentation as a technique of governance

In his theorizing on the relations between documentation and institutions, Ferraris (2013) emphasizes the indispensable role of documents in bureaucracy. According to him:

> Power is more capillary and effective today because we have seen a growth in the systems of registration, both in the weak documents (evidence gathering, control, hacking) and in the speed with which strong documents can be produced (delivery of acts, complex bureaucratic executions). Despite the illusions that once were fostered and the appearances of all times, the explosion of writing … has not led to an increase in emancipation but a growth in control, where the upside is an increase in rights because they are better documented.
>
> *(Ferraris, 2013, p. 271)*

Consequently, Ferraris (2013) argues that registering and documentation lay the foundation and are essential for governmentality, as theorized by Foucault. Therefore, we also apply the theories of governance and governmentality in this book (e.g. Foucault, 2007; Miller & Rose, 2008; Rose, 1996b, 1999a).

According to Foucault (1991), the exercise of modern political power is not based on a simplistic hierarchy of domination and subordination. It is not an issue of exercising discipline and control on someone. Instead, political power is based on conceptualizations, theories and ideas – that is, on knowledge – which are turned into practices and techniques of governance and power. With governmentality, he refers to

> … the ensemble formed by institutions, procedures, analyses, and reflections, calculations, and tactics that allow the exercise of this very specific, albeit very complex, power that has the population as its target, political economy as its major form of knowledge, and apparatuses of security as its essential technical instrument.
>
> *(Foucault, 2007, p. 108)*

Governmentality has led to the pre-eminence of the type of power that Foucault calls 'government' (Foucault, 2007, p. 108). However, government should not be considered as actions of a calculating political subject or as the operations of bureaucracy. It does not mean the work of individual politicians or specific governments in space and time. Rather, it refers to 'a certain way of striving to reach social and political ends by acting in a calculated manner upon the forces, activities and relations of the individuals that constitute the population' (Rose, 1999a, pp. 4–5). Since government has the population as its target, it is dependent on knowledge about it. According to Rose:

> … to govern a population one needs to isolate it as a sector of reality, to identify certain characteristics and processes proper to it, to make its features notable, speakable, writable, to account for them according to certain explanatory schemes. Government thus depends upon the production, circulation, organization, and authorization of truths that incarnate what is to be governed, which make it thinkable, calculable, and practicable.
>
> *(Rose 1999a, p. 6)*

Hence, government is dependent on calculations, registerings and categorizations of the population and its individuals; in short, it is contingent upon documentation in the production of which the knowledges of the 'psy' sciences (psychology, psychiatry, education, etc.) and their related institutions play a key role (Rose, 1999a). From this perspective, early education institutions can be seen as a practice of governance that attempts to maximize certain capacities of individuals and constrain others toward particular ends in accordance with their knowledges or 'regimes of truth' (cf. Foucault, 2007, p. 18; Rose, 1999a, pp. 182–204). They apply specific technologies – for example systematic documentation – that enable authorities to act upon the conduct of children and their parents individually and collectively (Miller & Rose, 2008, pp. 15–16).

However, applying the perspective of governance does not entail a negative notion of power. Instead, power is understood not only as a constraint to an individual but also as having benign potential and effects on human life. Besides, it is seen as a phenomenon that is always present in human interaction (e.g. Miller and Rose, 2008). Moreover, this approach to governance does not mean that there would not be opposition or 'resistance' to a particular regime of truths or practice of government. Human beings live their lives in a constant movement across different practices of government that subjectify them in different ways; that is, the different practices also aim at conducting their conduct according to controversial rationalities. Therefore, the existence of contestation and conflict in these practices is no surprise (Rose, 1996a, p. 35).

Governance should not be considered a phenomenon that takes its shape only within each nation state. Regimes of truth and the technologies of power are not (and have not been) restricted to the borders of individual states (e.g. Foucault, 2007), which can be seen, for example, in the spread of neoliberal thinking (Alasuutari & Qadir, forthcoming; Fejes & Dahlstedt, 2012). The same concerns ECE, its regimes of truth and technologies of power, for example the implementation of many of its documentation practices (e.g. Alasuutari & Alasuutari, 2012; Markström, 2009), which we consider as partly reflecting neoliberal thinking (see Harvey, 2005; Prasad, 2006). However, we do not assume that neoliberal or other transnational ideas and models would be applied in some 'pure' form at a national or institutional level. Instead, we consider the forms that the ideas and models take, for example concerning child documentation and assessment, as a result of domestication. This concept 'depicts a transformation in which a reform process initiated by references to exogenous models, ideas or catchwords ends up in people viewing the outcome as a unique domestic creation' (Alasuutari & Qadir, forthcoming). The process of domestication is not restricted to any special administrative field or hierarchy, but may originate and take place in a number of fields. For example, if domestication leads to reform in the form of a regulation or recommendation made at the national level (as has happened in the case of pedagogical documentation in Sweden), it often passes through several organizational levels all the way to the everyday life of individual citizens. In each context its implications are interpreted and negotiated. This means that the reform's effects may differ from what was originally planned. It also means that the new ideas are integrated as part of the discourses by which the specific practices are conceived and debated (Alasuutari & Alasuutari, 2012; Alasuutari & Qadir, forthcoming).

In all, the approach of governance and the concept of domestication imply that even though we examine child documentation in ECE by drawing on studies in the Nordic context, we consider our findings as both contextual and having relevance in other contexts. What will be discussed in this book reflects discourses and describes practices that have partly 'a local flavour'. At the same time, they also illuminate phenomena that are more universal in ECE.

The child and childhood as relational constructions

The theory of documentality and the approach of governance both imply that we cannot consider the child and childhood in essentialist or universal terms. Like all human beings, children have been and are constructed and subjectified in different and changing ways over the course of history, which is something they also participate in themselves (e.g. Rose, 1999a; Turmel, 2008; Vandenbroeck, Coussée & Bradt, 2010). In other words, we apply a constructionist understanding according to which notions of the child and childhood are thoroughly social, and historically and culturally produced and determined (e.g. James, Jenks & Prout 1998; Maybin, Woodhead, Moss, Dillon & Statham, 2000; Rogoff 2003).

Moreover, the notions of the child and childhood are fundamentally relational. This means that they are interdependent and mutually constitutive with the concepts of the adult and adulthood in a particular society (Alanen, 2009). For instance, children are often considered in terms of what they are not yet (capable of, allowed to do, etc.); that is, as 'becomings' (James & Prout, 1997). This means that they are rationalized in relation to the notions of what it means to be and act as an adult.

The conceptions of childhood and adulthood are produced and reproduced in intergenerational practices; in other words, in social practices and interactions taking place between members of existing generational categories. This applies also to other categorizations and social structurations, like gender, social class, 'race'/ethnicity and dis/ability, that shape the everyday lives, experiences and understandings of those human individuals identified terminologically as children (Alanen, 2009, pp. 161–2).

ECE forms a setting of intergenerational practices in which the notions of child and childhood – and respectively adult and adulthood and other categorizations – are negotiated. The negotiations and the constructions produced are, again, productive. They determine the educational institution: how its meaning and functions as well as the pedagogical work undertaken in it are understood and actualized (Dahlberg, Moss & Pence 2007, pp. 43–4). Woodhead (2005) phrases similar ideas in a somewhat different way. He argues that children, like adults, are cultural beings, and the same attribute applies to their relationship. Therefore, it would be misleading to conclude that any single pattern of nurturance, care and education were an essential pre-requisite for children's healthy development and a 'naturally' right way to fulfil these functions.

Child documentation can be seen as one example of the intergenerational practices of ECE in which notions of the child and adult as well as education are negotiated. Documentation produces a specific picture of the child, which we also examine in this book. Correspondingly, it implies what the adult – the parent and/or the educator – should be like. Thus, even though child documentation would only concern the child, it is intertwined with the conceptions of the adults in the child's life. Therefore, child documentation also has implications for the notions of parent and parenthood. Besides, as the story in the beginning of this chapter suggested, parents are also concretely involved in many ways in child documentation. Therefore we are also going to discuss parents and parenthood documentation practices.[1]

The empirical context

The chapters of this book draw on research that the authors have done individually and in collaboration with each other. The chapters present empirical examples and findings from studies that have been carried out mainly in Finland and Sweden, albeit some examinations also concern Danish and Norwegian ECE.[2] Additionally, we use international literature on ECE documentation as our material. Nevertheless, the ECE system of these four Nordic countries, and especially Finnish and Swedish early education, comprise our main knowledge base in this book.

In this book we will use the term early childhood education, abbreviated to ECE, as a generic concept to refer to the institutional education before children start compulsory education, which takes place at the age of seven in Finland and Sweden. By this choice we do not follow the traditions of any of the Nordic countries but try to avoid confusion, since in Denmark, Finland, Norway and Sweden partly different and partly the same terms are used, but with different meanings in reference to early education services. In Sweden, 'preschool' denotes the ECE services that are provided for children between one and five years. The six-year-olds enter 'a preschool class'. In the presentation of Swedish data we sometimes apply the term preschool as a synonym for ECE, for example, when the data is from a documentary source. In Finland, preschool refers to the same as preschool class in Sweden: this means, to the last year of early education before compulsory education. Finnish preschool is usually organized in 'day care' centres and sometimes at school. Day care is the colloquial term for ECE services in Finland. In English texts the concept early childhood education and care (abbreviated as ECEC) is a common label for these services.

In the Nordic countries, ECE is a universal and publicly-organized and/or subsidized service. Typically the child is entitled to ECE regardless of parental employment. Most often the ECE services are centre-based but there is also public family care available. It is often understood as a suitable form of care for children under two or three years. The data we present in this book has been collected in ECE centres that typically have a well-trained staff including members qualified both at tertiary level, like kindergarten teachers, and at lower level, like nursery nurses with a qualification at a secondary-school level (see Karila, 2012). In Finnish and Swedish ECE the staff work usually as a multi-professional team consisting of members with different educational backgrounds. The size of the 'child groups' for children over three years (the word 'class' is not used)[3] is around 20, and typically the groups have then three educators. The child groups consisting of younger children are often smaller and the adult–child ratio is bigger in them.

As a whole, ECE has a firm position in the welfare policies of the Nordic countries (see Karila, 2012; Kristjansson, 2006). Traditionally, ECE has been considered as compensating parental care while parents are working or studying. In recent decades, its importance in complementing parental care has been underlined, for example, by emphasizing its support for the child's development and lifelong learning. This is also reflected in the naturalization of the institutionalization of childhood; attending early education is expected in the Nordic countries, at least after the age of two or three (Karila, 2012). The pedagogical and educational role of ECE is also otherwise more prominent. For instance, in Finland and Sweden, ECE used to belong under the administration of social affairs but is nowadays part of the educational administration. This change will be highlighted also in the empirical analyses found in this book.

The organization of the book

The chapters of this book study documentation and assessment from three perspectives: (1) considering them as issues of curricula and pedagogy and as tasks of an educator; (2) studying them as negotiations on and about the child; and (3) examining them as actions on and of parents. The book is divided into different sections according to these perspectives.

The first part 'A view on curricula, didaktik and teachers' includes three chapters. Chapter 2, 'Assessment and documentation in the ECE curriculum: A focus on the Nordic tradition', discusses the basis of documentation and assessment in early education, the curriculum. Since it focuses on the Nordic curricula, it also illuminates the broader frame, in which the examinations of the following chapters are embedded. The Nordic tradition of curriculum design emphasizes children's performance and defines goals to strive for without specifying the objects of achievement. The other tradition to curricula design presented in the chapter, the Anglo-Saxon tradition, is characterized by the focus on the individual and by detailed formulations of goals to achieve for different age categories. The chapter discusses the contradictory tendencies of de- and re-centralization in the Nordic curricula, evident for example in the regulations and directions concerning documentation and assessment. It also argues that we can recognize a movement towards the Anglo-Saxon tradition of curriculum design in the Nordic countries.

Chapter 3, 'Different forms of documentation and assessment in ECE', familiarizes the reader with the documentation practices of Nordic early education at the grassroots level. Drawing on a case study of three Swedish preschools, it illuminates the types of documentation tools that are applied in ECE. It proposes that the documentation practices can best be characterized by the term 'multi-documentation'. The examination of the multi-documentation shows how the documentation tools comprise different forms of assessment, ranging from developmental-psychological, narrative and activity oriented assessments to self- and personality assessments. Finally, the chapter raises questions with regard to what sense the documentation and assessment practices are about empowering, supporting and strengthening children, parents and professionals, and to what sense they can weaken, mislead and constrain the different actors.

The fourth chapter, which ends the first part of the book, 'Teachers in intensified assessment and documentation practices: A didaktik approach', builds on the previous chapter and considers documentation and assessment practices and teachers' role in them from the viewpoint of a reflective, Continental didaktik approach. It approaches documents as co-actors in educational processes and focuses on the key question of the didaktik approach: why to assess, what is its function. The chapter introduces the concept of transformative assessment as a boundary object between different forms and functions of assessment and between micro-, meso- and macro-level actors in assessment and documentation practices. The preschool teachers' role can be described as trans-actors in the transformative multi-documentation and assessment.

The second part of the book, 'Auditing the child', shifts the focus to the social study of childhood and considers the notion of the child in documentation and assessment from two different starting points. Chapter 5, 'Documentation and listening to the children', begins its discussion from a common understanding of child documentation as a means to give children a 'voice'. By drawing on empirical data from parent–teacher discussions considering children's responses to specific questions, the chapter problematizes this notion. It argues that, despite its benevolent aims, listening to children through documentation is constrained by, and deeply embedded in, institutional and generational practices and assumptions about professionalism in ECE. Consequently, the child's view can be 'lost in translation'.

Chapter 6, 'The "normal" child', continues the discussion about the notions of the child by inviting the reader to consider how documentation and assessment practices produce normative ideas about the child and how these ideas are intertwined with the social order of the ECE institution. This order both controls and empowers the institutional actors in different ways. The chapter illustrates how the 'ordinary' or 'normal' child is produced in written documentation and in the intertwinement of text and talk. It also illuminates how the assessments and the normative function of documentation are predominantly implicit and actualized, especially when the child shows 'resistance' to the system of ECE or otherwise departs from its expectations.

The third part of the book, 'Focus on parenthood', consists of two chapters. Chapter 7, 'The governance and pedagogicalization of parents', highlights the demands on parents in the documentalized practices used to establish collaboration between the home and ECE. It considers practices and tools that are used to involve parents in the assessment and documentation of their child and the family. Through them, the parents are expected to embrace the ideas and discourses of the ECE institution. Furthermore, the documentalized practices yield unspoken expectations about how the parents should support their child in lifelong learning and how they can meet the institutional norms of good parenting.

Chapter 8, 'Parenthood between offline and online: About assessment and documentation', draws on 'netnographic' research on what parents write about assessment and documentation of children on Internet sites. In the discussions parents are free from the institutional constraints that are evident in, for example, parent–teacher meetings. The chapter considers whose interests seem to be involved in the discussions and who is assessing whom. Moreover, it considers in what ways the discussions can be seen both as empowering and constraining parenthood.

The final chapter, 'Dilemmas of assessment and documentation', ties together the key points of the preceding chapters and discusses the contradictions and tensions that are embedded in the assessment and documentation practices of Nordic ECE, regarding children, parents and professionals. It also considers the multidimensional steering and guiding of ECE documentation at the macro level, and proposes the concept of 'documentalized childhood' as capturing the function of this steering: childhood and the child that are essentially delineated, defined and produced in and by documentation.

Notes

1   In the book we use 'parent' and 'parents' alternately, often following the principle of simplicity in the text. When discussing data examples, the use of singular and plural forms depends on the particular example; who are the speakers in it or whom the example refers to. This means that with our choice of words – a parent or parents – we do not imply or make any statements about family compositions.

2   As will be shown in the other chapters of the book, the data consist of ECE documents at different levels (national, local, institutional, individual), Internet discussions, interviews with parents and professionals, and recordings of institutional interaction. In addition, our collaboration with ECE professionals in research and training provides us a continuing update on developments of the everyday practice. The research projects that this book draws on are the following:

Maarit Alasuutari: 'Standardizing Childhood? The Effects of Individual Plans for Early Childhood Education and Care', funded by the Academy of Finland (SA 116272); 'Documentality in Early Childhood Education', funded by the Research Collegium of University of Tampere.

Ann-Marie Markström: 'Preschool in transition a new childhood', funded by the Swedish Research Council; 'Parent–teacher conferences. Practices for constructions of childhood, parenthood and professionalization in the intermediate sphere between home and preschool', funded by the Swedish Research Council; 'Relations between home and preschool/school', funded by Linköping University.

Ann-Christine Vallberg-Roth: 'Steering by assessing children in systematic documentation – diverse normality' in the project 'Childhood in multiple contexts', funded by the Swedish council; 'Preschool teachers, parents and children in intensified documentation and assessment practices – documentality and transformative assessment as boundary object at micro, meso and macro level', funded by Malmö University, Centre for Profession Studies (CPS); 'Nordic comparative analysis of policy documents for preschool' – in Denmark, Finland, Iceland, Norway and Sweden – funded by the Nordic Council of Ministers and Ministry of Education and Research, Norway.

3   In Anglo-Saxon countries the word 'class' is often used to refer to a group of children. However, in Nordic early education the term 'child group' is used. 'Class' is primarily associated with school and older children, but it is also used in certain circumstances in the education of six-year-olds attending 'preschool'. The use of the term 'child group' is not merely contingent, but rather an ideological statement underlining the specific characteristics of Nordic ECE that demarcate it from school.

PART I

A view on curricula, didaktik and teachers

The first part of the book, with its three chapters, views assessment and documentation in ECE from a pedagogic perspective. However, it is not a toolkit of assessment and documentation, but a critical discussion of it. Assessment and documentation can be seen as fundamental pillars of educational practice, and this part of the book may support teachers to critically reflect on their choice of documentation tools. The foundations and the key regulations concerning assessment and documentation are usually collected in the curriculum. Therefore, in Chapter 2 the reader will be acquainted with the Nordic and Anglo-Saxon traditions of curriculum design. The focus, though, is on the Nordic curricula and how they regulate documentation and assessment in ECE. We will also consider whether we can still talk about a 'pure' or 'singular' model of Nordic curricula. In Chapter 3 we turn to the 'grass roots' level of ECE and examine different types of documentation tools, ranging from open documentation to standardized methods. We propose that the collection of documentation practices in ECE can be characterized by the term 'multi-documentation', which is intermingled with various forms of assessment. Chapter 4 focuses on the question: what is the function of multi-documentation, what is its purpose? As a summary of the discussion in the first part of the book, this chapter introduces the concept of transformative assessment and the teacher as a multi- or trans-actor within it.

2

ASSESSMENT AND DOCUMENTATION IN THE ECE CURRICULUM

A focus on the Nordic tradition

We are living in an age of measurement, and typical notions of our time are quality assurance, customer satisfaction and evidence, as well as the focus on objectives, results and the key competences that every citizen is considered to need. In a global knowledge economy, human development and education is seen as the key to economic growth; moreover, intensifying international competition has also shifted the focus to younger children. In the report 'Starting Strong III' (OECD, 2012) the Organization for Economic Co-operation and Development (OECD), an important agent in the development of early education internationally, argues that high quality investments in early childhood education (ECE) provide higher long-term economic returns than investments in later forms of schooling.

As key means of developing ECE, the OECD presents national curricula (OECD, 2001, 2006, 2012). According to this, the curriculum and learning standards can ensure the quality of diverse ECE activities, help staff to develop pedagogical strategies, and help parents to make informed choices and better understand child development. Indeed, the OECD project 'Starting Strong' (ibid.) has contributed to the development of ECE curricula in many countries. Currently, most of the OECD countries[1] apply ECE curricula, at least for the older children, but there is a growing interest in also formulating curricula for the youngest children in ECE (OECD, 2012). All the Nordic countries have designed an ECE curriculum covering all the years before primary education.

In this chapter, we present two traditions of curriculum design in ECE: the Anglo-Saxon tradition and the Nordic tradition. We also take a closer look at the Nordic ECE curricula and how they guide and regulate documentation. Since the curriculum composes the official frame for assessment and documentation in ECE, this chapter also depicts the Nordic ECE system at a general level and, hence, illuminates the context of the discussions in the following chapters.

Before moving to the characteristics of the two main curriculum traditions in ECE, we briefly define what is meant by a national curriculum. After the presentation of the Anglo-Saxon and Nordic traditions of curriculum design, we take a closer look at how the Nordic curricula are constructed and how they steer documentation and assessment in ECE. We end the chapter with remarks concerning the recent transnational trends of the Nordic curricula.

Curriculum at the national level

Generally, a curriculum at the national level can be seen as a common framework including principles, goals, guidelines and standards that the authorities want to communicate to citizens, educational staff, parents and students (Bennett, 2010; Vallberg-Roth, 2006). Fundamental values such as democracy, justice, diversity, equality and other foundations that should be supported by the educational institutions are discussed. In ECE, the curriculum points out the key goals of early education and refers principally to the contents (what to teach) and to the methods or the pedagogy (how to teach) to be used to support the children's development and learning (OECD, 2012). In practice, the curriculum provides guidelines for, or stipulates, the functioning of ECE; hence, it aims to ensure the quality and consistency of education and to meet the needs of different children on a local level. Moreover, it often facilitates parental involvement in ECE, a goal also emphasized in the Starting Strong reports (OECD, 2001, 2006, 2012). Furthermore, the curriculum at the national level gives the framework for, or motivates, documentation and assessment in ECE.

Let us consider an example from Finnish early childhood education. The first national curriculum for ECE in Finland (Stakes, 2004) underlined parental knowledge of the child and introduced partnership as a general frame for parent–practitioner collaboration. As a consequence, many Finnish municipalities developed new collaboration practices to be implemented in ECE. A 'beginning' meeting with the parents is one example of these; the purpose is to collect information about the child when he/ she first enters an ECE centre. Typically, the municipalities also developed a form to be filled out in the meeting with the parent(s). Hence, the ideal and principle of partnership motivated the implementation of a new documentation tool.

The initial ('beginning') meeting exemplifies how the everyday documentation in ECE is linked with the national curriculum. In the curriculum, the guidance can be more general and can be expressed as ideals, as in the Finnish example above. The curriculum can also include more exact regulations, such as general offer of language screening for all three-year-old children in ECE in Denmark. Hence, the national curricula differ in the way they orientate and regulate the everyday practices of education. However, it is clear that there is an increasing international interest in the relationships between national curricula, assessment and family involvement (OECD, 2012).

The differences of national curricula are related to different factors, such as economy, education system and tradition. They also balance diverse expectations from different stakeholders (OECD, 2012). Hence, ideals, ideologies, values and other factors permeate the formulations of curricula. This means that curricula are characterized and influenced by various factors as well as by explicit and implicit purposes. These are interlinked with different discourses about children, childhood and early childhood institutions, which have also changed throughout history. It is important to keep this in mind when we analyse curricula.

Two traditions of curriculum design

In ECE, we can differentiate two types of curriculum design. These often are labelled either as the Nordic tradition and the Anglo-Saxon tradition or as the social pedagogical approach and the infant school approach. Bennett (2010) describes the two approaches in the following manner:

1. The social pedagogical approach of curriculum design is characterized by a short and non-detailed text that focuses on the whole child and on education that consists of both care and education (the idea of educare). However, the emphasis and interest is not on child outcomes or measures. This approach is used in the Nordic countries and in some Eastern European countries.
2. The infant school approach focuses on the child's readiness for school. The curriculum is more detailed than in the social pedagogical approach and shows an interest in measuring individual children.

Hence, the Nordic or social pedagogical tradition of curriculum design is characterized by more comprehensive aims and broader developmental goals. More specific academic approaches and the focus on cognitive development are again typical for the infant school or Anglo-Saxon approach (Bennett, 2010). Consequently, the two approaches are also grounded in and produce different notions of the child and childhood as well as different understandings of an early education centre, as shown in Table 2.1, which describes the two approaches in more detail.

The differences between the Anglo-Saxon and the Nordic tradition of curriculum design also imply different interests in documentation. The more academic Anglo-Saxon tradition focuses on the individual and emphasizes outcomes; therefore, detailed and standardized goals of achievement, usually targeting cognitive development, are formulated for different age categories. Documentation should concern the assessment of the target areas. The Nordic tradition, with its more comprehensive approach, focuses on inputs and describes children's performance in terms of goals without specifying the objects of achievement (OECD, 2012, p.1). It also defines what is expected from the staff. The documentation is then supposed to be used not only to illustrate children's development but also to illuminate the teachers' work and the conditions for children's learning.

TABLE 2.1 Features of two curricular traditions

	Preschool as preparation for school	The Nordic tradition
Understandings of the child and childhood	The child is a young person to be formed, as a literate, compliant well-behaved student... Education is conceived as an investment in the future of society. State and adult purposes are fore grounded. Pedagogy is focussed on 'useful' learning, readiness for school... A tendency to privilege indoors learning.	The child as a subject of rights: to autonomy, well-being... and the right to growth on the child's own premises. The child as agent of her own learning, a rich child with natural learning and research strategies... An outdoors child of pleasure and freedom. A time for childhood that can never be repeated.
The early childhood centre	Generally (though by no means always), the centre is seen as a service based on individual demand, a matter of 'choice' for the individual parents. It is viewed as a place for individual development, learning and instruction. Children will be expected to reach pre-defined levels of learning (goals to be achieved at each stage).	The centre is seen as a public socioeducational service, in which the community interest – as well as the interests of individual parents – must be taken into account. It is viewed as a life space, a place in which children and pedagogues learn "to be, to know, to do and to live together" (Delors Report, 1996). The elasticity of child development and learning is recognised.
Curriculum development	Frequently, a prescribed ministerial curriculum, with detailing of goals and outcomes is proposed. Assumption that the curriculum can be 'delivered' by the individual teacher in a standardised way whatever the group or setting.	A broad national guideline, with a devolution of curriculum and its implementation to municipalities and the centres. Responsibility falls on the centre staff, a collegial responsibility... A culture of research and observation on children's interests and how they learn.
Focus of programme	A focus on learning and skills, especially in areas useful for school readiness. Mainly teacher directed (Weikart et al., 2003). Teacher-child relationships may be instrumentalised through large numbers of children per teacher an the need to achieve detailed curriculum goals.	Focus on working with the whole child and the family – broad developmental goals as well as learning are pursued. Programmes are child-centred – interactivity with educators and peers encouraged and the quality of life in the institution is given high importance.
Pedagogical strategies	A balanced mix of instruction, child initiated activities and thematic work is encouraged, managed by each teacher. The national curriculum must be 'delivered' correctly. Where children are concerned, an emphasis is placed on individual autonomy and self-regulation.	The national curriculum guides the choice of pedagogical themes and projects. Confidence is placed in the teachers' professionalism and in the child's own learning strategies, that is, on learning through relationships, through play and through educator scaffolding at the appropriate moment.

Targets and goals for children	Prescribed targets – often focussing on learning areas, such as emergent literacy and cognitive development – may be set at national level to be reached in all centres, sometimes translated by each year of age.	Broad orientations rather than prescribed outcomes. Goals are to be striven for, rather than achieved. A diffusion of goals may be experienced, with diminished accountability unless quality is actively pursued.
Indoor and outdoor spaces for young children	The indoors is considered to be the primary learning space, and resources are focussed here. Outdoors is generally seen as an amenity, a recreational area and perhaps as important for health and motor development.	Indoors and outdoors have equal pedagogical importance. Much thought and investment given to the organization of outdoor space and its use. Young children may spend 3 or 4 hours daily out of doors and in organised visits. The environment and its protection is generally an important theme.
Assessment	Learning outcomes and assessment often required, at least on entry into primary school. Goals for the group are clearly defined. Graded assessment of each child with respect to pre-defined competences may be an important part of the teacher's role.	Formal assessment not required. Broad developmental goals are set for each child by negotiation (educator–parent–child). Goals are informally evaluated unless screening is necessary. Multiple assessment procedures are favoured.
Quality control	Quality control based on clear objectives and frequently, on pre-defined learning outcomes. Standardised testing may be used in programme evaluation, but in most centres, child testing is not allowed. Assessment of skills mastery is generally ongoing and the responsibility of the lead teacher. An external inspectorate may also visit centres, but may be under-staffed (especially in child care) or staffed by personnel without training in ECEC pedagogy.	Quality control is more participatory, based on educator and team responsibility and, depending on country, supervised by parent boards and municipalities. Documentation used not only to mark child progress but also as collegial research on staff pedagogical approaches. A wide range of child outcomes may be sought, and assessed informally in multiple ways. External validation undertaken by municipal pedagogical advisors and/or inspectors. The focus is on centre performance rather than on child assessment.

Source: Bennett (2010).

There are studies that point out that a combination of these two curriculum models can be beneficial both in the short and the long term (e.g. Sheridan, Pramling Samuelsson & Johansson, 2009). The comprehensive model is most likely to improve a child's creativity, independence, self-confidence, initiative, motivation to learn and long-term outcomes. The academic model is most likely to improve a child's literacy, numeracy, specific knowledge and short-term outcomes (OECD, 2012). In the present day Nordic ECE, both of these traditions coexist, but there seems to be a growing interest in the individual child's skills and knowledge.

The Nordic ECE curricula: similar and different

Overall, when it comes to the ECE curricula for one- to five-year-olds in the Nordic countries – Denmark, Finland, Norway and Sweden – and their content construction, a pattern appears in terms of uniformity with variation (Åsén & Vallberg-Roth, 2012; Vallberg-Roth, 2011b, 2013a). Some basic similarities are shown, but the curricula also differ in part and do not have quite the same character.

All the Nordic curricula for ECE are built into decentralized management systems, which mean management by objectives. In addition to the national curriculum, municipalities and ECE settings have their own policy documents, plans or curricula that broaden and specify the ideas of the national curriculum and concretize the educational work at the local level following the lines articulated in the national curriculum. Hence, the local ECE documents supplement and operate in parallel with the national guidelines in ECE settings. Moreover, the ECE documents of different administrative levels are intertextual. They are shaped in reference to official upper-level documents and formulations and, naturally, to other texts, such as disciplinary literature.

Each of the ECE curricula of the Nordic countries specifies some content areas of early education (see Table 2.2), the labels of which correspond to school subjects. The content areas are partly similar, but there are also differences. For example, there is 'nature and science' in all curricula, while 'mathematics' is not present in the Danish curriculum. 'Technology' is specifically emphasized in the Swedish and Norwegian curricula, while 'body and movement' is emphasized in the Danish and Norwegian curricula. Regarding religion and conviction, there is another kind of division: 'Ethics, religion and philosophy' and 'religious-philosophical orientation' are a part of the Norwegian and Finnish curricula but not emphasized in the Danish and Swedish curricula. In addition, Norway has explicitly inscribed Christian and humanistic values in the law on early education and care (Vallberg-Roth, 2013a). We can assume that this has to do, for example, with differences in the population of the four countries, and thus with cultural diversity. Finally, Finland is the only country that has the 'historical-societal' content in its curriculum. However, it does not define language as one of its 'orientations'; instead, the role of language is discussed from a holistic perspective and is considered to cover transversely all substantive orientations and ECE activities (see Stakes, 2004).

With regard to the nature of the goals, the Swedish curriculum for preschool presents only goals to strive for regarding the ECE activities that should be interpreted and translated at the municipal and local levels (Vallberg-Roth, 2006). The goal areas of the curriculum are constructed according to the main content areas (see Table 2.2). In a similar manner, the Finnish curriculum does not define goals for children to achieve, but goals for the preschool to strive for (Vallberg-Roth, 2013a). However, the goal-setting does not follow the orientations – that is, content areas – of the curriculum; rather, it is defined as the promotion of the child's personal well-being, reinforcement of considerate behaviour and action towards others, and gradual build-up of the child's autonomy (Stakes, 2004, p.14). Nevertheless, in practice, the universal use of individual educational plans (IEPs) as a documentation tool in Finnish ECE can lead to setting individual goals for children to achieve (see Alasuutari & Karila, 2010).

TABLE 2.2 The content areas and documentation in the Nordic ECE policy

Country	Content	Documentation/individual level
Denmark	Comprehensive development Language screening for three-year-olds Children's social skills Language Body and movement Nature and natural phenomena Cultural expression and values	Language screening for three-year-olds
Finland	Mathematical Science Historical-societal Aesthetic Ethical Religious-philosophical	Individual Educational Plans (IEPs)
Norway	Communication, language and text Body, movement and health Art, culture and creativity Ethics, religion and philosophy Immediate environment and society Nature, environment and technology Number, place and form	Language assessment for children
Sweden	Main goal areas like Norms and Values, Development and Learning (including Language-Communication, Mathematics, Science and Technology) Children's influence Cooperation with the home and school, and follow-up, evaluation and development	Systematic documentation of each child's learning and development

In Denmark, the goal setting is decentralized to the local level. ECE settings can formulate their curriculum after the six nationally regulated themes listed in Table 2.2. Although the Danish Act on ECE focuses on the education and pedagogy of the institutions and not on the individual child's skills, the national definitions and aims can be transformed locally into different types of goal formulations, both as goals for children to achieve at the individual level and goals to strive for at the preschool activity level (Åsén & Vallberg-Roth, 2012). The Norwegian curriculum for ECE is also non-specific in its formulation of goals; however, the goals are more set as objectives to strive for rather than objectives to achieve (i.e., requirements). The goal areas are defined according to the main content areas of the Norwegian curriculum.

In setting goals, all the Nordic curricula seem to focus on the work of the institutions and not on the individual child's skills. However, as a result of the decentralized organization, this focus can be locally transformed and translated into different types of goal formulations, both as goals for children to achieve at the individual level and goals to strive for at the preschool activity level. This transformation is partly supported by the regulation of documentation in the curricula of the four Nordic countries.

Documentation and evaluation in the Nordic curricula

Running parallel to the decentralized organization, there also seems to be an increased tendency towards re-centralized control of ECE. This is shown especially in the national demands of documentation and assessment. The policy documents of the four Nordic countries either have specific sections on evaluation and documentation or discuss them in relation to other topics. Evaluation and documentation are considered both at the local level concerning ECE setting and municipalities, and at the level of individual children.

The guidelines for planning, documentation and evaluation in the Norwegian curriculum provide us with an illuminating example concerning the steering of documentation and evaluation at the local level. In Norway, each ECE setting is free to choose the methods and scope of documentation and assessment in relation to local conditions and needs. All settings shall also prepare an annual plan. They can also decide the extent to which there should be designed plans for shorter periods. Documentation of staff's work and children's learning are mentioned as a means to get different views regarding activities and to open up a critical reflective practice. The Norwegian curriculum also prescribes that ECE settings will not usually assess whether individual children achieve goals in relation to given criteria. However, this can be seen as contradictory as regards the general offer of language assessment for children introduced in Norway in 2010.

In a similar manner, the Finnish curriculum (Stakes, 2004) emphasizes decision-making, planning and continuous evaluation at the municipal and institutional level by demanding a municipal and unit-specific ECE plan or curriculum. However, there is no specific section concerning evaluation in the Finnish curriculum; instead, evaluation is mentioned in connection with the role of parents.

Their right to participate in the planning of the unit's activities is stated, as is their involvement in drafting and evaluating the child's individual educational plan (IEP), which should be drafted for each child in Finnish ECE. Staff are expected to systematically and consciously observe the child for this plan. Otherwise, the instructions about the IEP plan are very general (Stakes, 2004).

Furthermore, the Swedish curriculum prescribes systematic documentation at the individual level concerning both the institution and individual children. Overall, the Swedish as well as the Danish curricula focus more on evaluation than on planning at the unit level. For example, in Denmark the ECE institutions must account for the effects, and they condition possible funding (cf. Hjort, 2008), which was not previously the case. This shift means that the control of the Danish ECE runs from collective goals to individual goals (ibid). According to Hjort (2008), the justification for this change is that there should be democratic insight into what taxpayers get for their money. Meanwhile, there are some very specific challenges. These extra challenging goal areas include the integration of children with refugee and migration background and the work to break the social heritage. One way Denmark has responded to these challenges has been the implementation of obligatory offer of language screening for three-year-olds. According Jensen, Broström and Hansen (2010), the democratic dimension of the Danish ECE is relatively strong, but currently constructed in a framework of tests and specializations (e.g. in key competences). Political discussions on the content of the ECE curriculum and its implementation are framed by a control system based on optimizing the pedagogical practice in relation to standardized objectives and results orienting to the individual level.

All four of the Nordic curricula are also witnessing a trend moving from care, play and learning to highlighting learning and knowledge in specific areas and evaluation linked to lifelong learning (cf. Vallberg-Roth, 2011b). Although the curricula underline the evaluation at the unit level (regarding, for example, the activities), the evaluation and assessment also concern and move to the individual level. There are also more specific examples concerning the changing trend, for instance, the demands to systematically document and evaluate children's learning and knowledge in content areas such as language, mathematics and science in Sweden (cf. Bennett, 2010). Hence, breakthroughs from the Anglo-Saxon tradition of evaluation begin to assert themselves in today's Nordic ECE curricula, and we can see a coexistence of the two traditions. The movement appears to be motivated by the aims of strengthening the economic competitiveness of the nation and its economic growth. It also follows the suggestions of the European Union (EU). To meet the global challenges of society and a knowledge economy, the EU formulates key competencies that every citizen will need in lifelong learning (European Communities, 2007). Acquiring skills in specific areas – especially language, mathematics, science and technology, meta-cognitive learning, social skills, cultural awareness and entrepreneurship – are emphasized in relation to global competition. Thus, the EU's key competences for lifelong learning are more focused on succeeding in later school years and working life than on the care, play and well-being of early education (Åsén & Vallberg-Roth, 2012). Referring to Gert Biesta (2009, 2011), we can ask whether the 'leaning' on the content areas in contemporary Nordic curricula reflects the phenomenon of 'learnification', that is, a general trend towards the individual's increasing responsibility for lifelong learning. Biesta (2011) points out that learning is fundamentally an individualistic term referring to what people do as individuals. It stands in contrast to the concept of education that always indicates a relationship: Someone educates someone else, and those who educate have a certain sense of purpose for their activities. With the emphasis on lifelong learning, there is, arguably, a wider scope for adult-normed content and adult-normed assessment in the Nordic ECE.

Curricula, documentation and assessment

In this chapter, we have presented two traditions of ECE curriculum design: the Anglo-Saxon tradition and the Nordic tradition. We have also looked more carefully at the national curricula of the four Nordic countries. In the steering of education, the national curricula present the ideological system that also includes, for example, the definitions of the objectives and content of education. Moreover, steering is also exercised legally and financially as well as by monitoring and evaluating through control systems. Naturally, the different systems also overlap. For example, IEPs can be seen as 'curricula at an individual level'. At the same time, they can be understood as expressions of contemporary regulation in a borderland of legal, ideological and control systems that are related to the state, municipality (or local institutions), professionals and users as actors (cf. Alasuutari & Alasuutari, 2012). In the decentralized education system, the control and assessment of the results of the local ECE will be more important when it comes to maintaining a national equivalence and standard. Consequently, on the one hand, there is decentralization, and, on the other, there is a re-centralization through increased control, that is, through documentation and assessment (cf. Lindensjö & Lundgren, 2000).

There is also a trend towards increased goal and outcome rationality, individualization and harmonization in the Nordic ECE (cf. Andersen-Østergaard, Hjort & Skytthe-Kaarsberg-Schmidt, 2008). Goal- and outcome-orientation can seem to be more vague in ECE when compared with other forms of education, but language tests, different means of quality control, and adjusting the EU's key competences for lifelong learning in the curriculum may be seen as examples of goal- and outcome-orientation. For example, individualization is reflected in documentation such as language assessments for children in Denmark and Norway and in IEPs in Finland. Harmonization is implied in more comparable, consistent and standardized evaluation criteria. Examples of this are harmonization through content definitions and documentation requirements, such as unit-specific curricula. This movement is seen as characteristic of governance in accordance with the New Public Management (NPM). Generally, the focus on the performance management and quality assurance with children and parents as users (customers) are seen as part of a long-term influence of NPM (cf. Andersen-Østergaard et al., 2008). This has led to market-orientation focusing on the management of economic prioritization and control as well as evaluation models inspired by the private sector.

Consequently, we can recognize the implementation of transnational ideas and a move towards the Anglo-Saxon model of curriculum design in the Nordic ECE curricula. As explained in the introduction of this chapter, we do not see these processes as straightforward developments; rather, we consider them a domestication process, the results of which may differ considerably from the original ideas and models (Alasuutari & Qadir, forthcoming). The frames and regulations that the curricula provide for assessment and documentation in ECE experience several 'translations' as they are implemented at the 'grass-roots' level. The next chapters will illuminate these translations in Finnish and Swedish ECE.

Note

1   There are 34 member countries in the OECD. Besides most European countries, they include among others the USA, Canada, Australia, New Zealand, Japan, Israel and Chile. When this book was being written negotiations about the membership of Russia were topical in the OECD.

3

DIFFERENT FORMS OF DOCUMENTATION AND ASSESSMENT IN ECE

As was already pointed out in the introduction, we can find a multitude of documentation in present-day early childhood education (ECE). Documentation can apply different means, both electronic and non-electronic, for example, video and sound recordings, photographs and written materials. As will be shown, documentation can also include different forms ranging from open and fairly unspecified registering to structured and focused tools. Additionally, its focus and contents can vary.

In this chapter, we will give examples of different forms of documentation in ECE. Our interest is in documentation that concentrates on children and on the activities in ECE. We will consider how assessment is interwoven in different forms of documentation and what this assessment is about. We will also discuss to what extent the different forms of documentation and assessment can, on the one hand, empower, support and strengthen children, parents and professionals. On the other hand, we will examine the extent to which the different forms of documentation and assessment can weaken, mislead and restrict these actors. To give an example of the variety of different forms and tools of documentation and assessment, we will start by presenting findings from a Swedish study (Vallberg-Roth, 2012b).

Multi-documentation – case example

Our case example is based on three preschools in Sweden (see Vallberg-Roth, 2012b). At first glance, the preschools seem to differ from each other in their pedagogical approaches because of their different profiles. The first preschool is inspired by the ideas of Reggio Emilia (Dahlberg, Moss & Pence, 1999) and works with pedagogical documentation. According to its website, the second preschool emphasizes the notion that children are unique individuals; this is put into practice by using an individual development plan (IDP) for each child. The third preschool, which is located in the countryside, has a health profile and is certified for its environmental efforts. According to its website, this preschool works with portfolios. Notwithstanding the contrasts between all of the preschools, they have one aspect in common: they apply more extensive documentation than they present on their websites.

This is revealed in the interviews in which the teachers give long lists of different documentation tools. They talk, for example, about pedagogical documentation and portfolios, including both teacher and child folders. In the preschool with a profile inspired by Reggio Emilia, the pedagogical documentation includes depictions of the child's creative activities, her or his knowledge of nature, language competence and socio-emotional development. In the preschool emphasizing that children are unique individuals, the child folders describe each child as a person as well as describing the child's project materials and the child's interviews. The teachers also bring up learning stories and IDPs as documentation tools. In addition, they discuss different forms of parent questionnaires that they apply in their work. Moreover, the interviews reveal that a number of standardized documentation methods and programmes for social and emotional development are used in the three preschools. In all, they show the wide-ranging and extensive nature of documentation in the everyday life of the ECE institutions (see Table 3.1 and associated notes). We call this phenomenon *multi-documentation*.

TABLE 3.1 The documentation tools of the three preschools

Preschool with a profile inspired by Reggio Emilia	Preschool in which children are seen as unique individuals	Preschool with a health profile
• Pedagogical documentation • Social and Emotional Training (SET)[1] • Second Step[2] • Individual Development Plans (IDPs) • Parent questionnaires • Electronic documentation (as pedagogical documentation and children's creations on the web)	*(1) The teacher's folder including* • IDPs • Relationship Development Scheme (RUS)[3] • Step sheets for different fields of knowledge[4] • Pedagogical documentation • Parental form • Electronic photo frames *(2) The child's folder including* • Portfolio with a description of the child as a person • Theme and project materials (learning stories) • Interview questions	• Portfolio (learning stories) • Diary (everyday group activities) • START[5] • TRAS[6] • Second Step • Health care-documents • Parent questionnaires • Electronic photo frames • Documentation for health and environmental council

Overall, it seems that the documentation in the three preschools focuses on children and parents as well as on teachers, yet the majority of the material is designed for teachers with a gaze on the child. However, some teachers reported in the interviews that they would rather focus the documentation on small groups of children than on individual children (Vallberg-Roth, 2012b).

The documentation applied in the three preschools, such as pedagogical documentation and learning stories, also seems to be quite open. According to Gjems (2010), most of the documentation can be categorized as observation, analysis methods, or as falling between these two methods. The third type of documentation, tests, is more rare. Observations are fairly open, and they can focus either on one child or on several children. The teacher decides the focus, time and situation for the observation, such as when children participate in a project. The observations are usually documented in a written form, but they can also be supplemented by photographs as well as by audio and video recordings. Analysis (mapping, monitoring) is more easily associated with assessment than observations; it uses a diagram or scheme with predefined categories about particular sub-skills. Documentation is limited to these sub-skills, for example, what the child masters in various linguistic areas, such as vocabulary, language and comprehension. The step sheets used in the second preschool in our study could fall into this group. Testing is an even more specific and detailed documentation and assessment method. Tests address specific sub-areas and relate a child's performance to standardized scales, typically to the mean results of children of the same age. Tests are usually administered in a separate room outside the child's daily environment and by following a similar protocol with every child. Most tests require the test leader to have a specific qualification (Gjems, 2010). TRAS would be closest to the tests in our case example, even though it has also aspects of analysis.

In all, it is difficult to demarcate or exclusively categorize the different forms of documentation in the three preschools. Consequently, the various aspects of assessment that are intertwined with them can appear blurry. Next, we will take a closer look at some of the forms of documentation listed above and consider them in relation to assessment. For our discussion we have selected documentation tools that are applied in broader contexts, not just in Sweden.

Pedagogical documentation, portfolio and IDP

The use of *pedagogical documentation* is well established and widespread in early childhood education (OECD, 2012). Although the idea and practice of pedagogical documentation has a long history, it is mostly associated with the early childhood institutions of Reggio Emilia (Dahlberg, Moss & Pence, 2007). Pedagogical documentation underlines the interconnectedness and the process of analysis, reflection and interpretation (Dahlberg, Moss & Pence, 1999). It is described as an evaluation tool that permits activities to develop in which children's development and learning are examined in relation to a group of children, the environment and teachers' approaches (Bjervås, 2011). Pedagogical documentation is actually referring both to the process and to the content. As content, it refers to what children are doing and saying, to the work of the children, and to how the teacher relates to the children and their work. The actual material can take many forms, including handwritten notes, photographs, audio recordings and computer graphics. It makes the pedagogical work audible and concrete. As a process, pedagogical documentation involves the use of the material as a means to reflect upon the pedagogical work. The reflection can be done by the teacher alone or together with other teachers, children, parents or politicians (Dahlberg et al., 1999).

Pedagogical documentation is often associated with democratic expectations. It aims at both educational practices within the institution as well as the position of education in the wider society:

> We have presented pedagogical documentation as a vital tool for the creation of a reflective and democratic pedagogical practice. /.../ Pedagogical documentation also contributes to the democratic project of the early childhood institution /.../ Through making pedagogical work both visible and a subject for democratic and open debate, pedagogical documentation provides the possibility of early childhood institutions gaining a new legitimacy in society.
>
> *(Dahlberg et al., 1999, p. 145)*

Pedagogical documentation can be one tool for showcasing the actual practice of ECE, opening it up for a review (Åsén & Vallberg-Roth, 2012). The primary function of pedagogical documentation is that it forms a basis for reflection among teachers. Documentation can only be considered pedagogical if someone reflects upon it. However, pedagogical documentation can also be seen as a social construction by which teachers, through their choices of what is worth documenting, are co-builders in a selective and biased process; 'the descriptions we make and the categories we apply, just like the interpretations we use to understand what is happening, are permeated by silent conventions, classifications and categories' (Colliander, Stråhle & Wehner-Godée, 2010, p. 13). Accordingly, pedagogical documentation can be presented not only as documentation for emancipation and resistance (Lenz-Taguchi, 2000) but also as a risky method. Risks can emerge both through the classifications and categories that teachers use and through which they exercise power and control, thereby influencing the child's identity construction (Dahlberg et al., 1999).

We can also ask if pedagogical documentation is always in line with the assumptions of the curriculum. In Sweden, there is an example of this: the guidelines from the National Agency for Education in Sweden (Skolverket, 2012) prescribe pedagogical documentation as a relational tool to be applied in preschools. Learning is not seen as an individual and independent activity but as something that is interconnected with other people and the surrounding environment. The pedagogical documentation is linked to the concept of rhizome and to the views of post-humanist scholars by referring to the physicist Barad (2003). The guidelines state:

The concept of rhizome is borrowed from biology and refers to a plant-root system. The system can grow and spread in different directions, unlike, for example, a tree root that always branches at the ends. A rhizomatic thinking makes it possible to describe how learning, like rhizomes, takes unpredictable paths, and is in no way linear or progressive. The learning does not follow a linear, pre-mapped route, but goes a little back and forth in unpredictable paths.

(Skolverket, 2012, p. 27)

The post-humanistic approach and the use of rhizomes as an ideal raises questions about how linear management systems, with predetermined directions in the form of curricula with set objectives, can be linked with the required pedagogical documentation based on nonlinear ideals, such as rhizomes. Conflicting features can be seen between democratic claims and the prescribed rhizomatic ideal in the agency's guidelines (Skolverket, 2012) since the rhizomes can be described as both the best and the worst (Deleuze & Guattari, 1987, pp. 9–10). Even fascism can be mentioned in this context: Deleuze and Guattari argue that a rhizomatic process can also grow in an undemocratic direction (1987, p. 9). Likewise, it can be asked whether the goals of a curriculum (which puts the human in the centre) are congruous with the post-humanistic and non-anthropocentric ideals of the type of pedagogical documentation prescribed in the agency's guidelines (see Vallberg-Roth, 2013a).

The *portfolio* is another widely used and well-known documentation tool in ECE (OECD, 2012), as well as at other levels of education. Like pedagogical documentation, it is also associated with democratic practice because of its emphasis on student participation. A portfolio provides students with an opportunity to influence and take responsibility for their own learning as regards goal setting, planning, documentation, reflection and assessment (Jungkvist & Sandell, 2002).

A portfolio comprises of a compilation of a student's work and intends to show the student's efforts, progress and study results in a specific area or areas (Lindström, 2011). In ECE, a meta-cognitive perspective often motivates the use of portfolios, which allow students to see and influence their own development. This is also shown in the example below, a quotation from the website of a Swedish preschool.

My Book (Portfolio)

The portfolio approach to documentation clearly gets children to:

See their own performance

Take greater responsibility for their own learning

See and influence their own development

Be viewed as individuals

Strengthen their self-esteem

Stimulate the desire for lifelong learning.

As in our example, portfolios can also include *learning stories*. Learning stories are a narrative mode of documenting children's learning in order to make learning more accessible to children, parents and teachers. A learning story may combine photographs with stories about the child, as in the following Swedish example:

> During the theme, we have talked about the size, appearance, difference and similarities between different trees, been searching for different trees and talked even more. We have expanded our vocabulary and practicing our conceptualization with the tree as a starting point. /.../ In the photo, Ben made pear prints in various colours pasted up on the magic tree. /.../ Ben has made two trees, one large and one small. I'm in the photograph and I have two sticks in my hands. A short pin and one long.

Learning stories are founded in a sociocultural and situated viewpoint (Carr & Lee, 2012). The sociocultural perspective looks at learning and knowledge not primarily as representations in the child's mind but as a relationship between an individual with both body and mind and an environment in which the individual feels, thinks and interacts. The narratives allow for constructing learner identities. It is through narratives and story telling that the teacher, parent and child create and recreate the selfhood and learning identities as expressions of our culture (Carr & Lee, 2012).

From a critical perspective, the portfolio and learning stories may be seen as part of a hidden curriculum and governance as they presume the child's reflection on her or his own learning. In this self-governmental technology, children learn to be generous with their inner beings (Gustafsson, 2004). With the introduction of logbooks, portfolios, individual assessment methods and so forth, children are governed to actively take responsibility for their own learning and for assessing their own efforts (e.g. Kampmann, 2005). These methods require a high degree of self-reflection in which children are expected to inform their deliberations, internal sensations, feelings and things they can improve on in the future.

The third (open) tool for documentation that had a salient position in two preschools in our case study is the *individual developmental plan* (IDP), which can be seen as 'a curriculum at an individual level' (see also Chapter 2). IDPs are plans that are drafted for all children in Swedish schools, but they are not obligatory in preschools.[7] This is also reflected in our case example: IDPs were not used in one of the preschools in our study. The IDP was introduced to the Swedish education system both to enable more students to achieve the national goals set in the curricula and syllabi and to enable students and parents to have more influence on the content of student work at school.

However, research shows both that IDPs do not regularly meet their aims and that parents do not have much influence on them (e.g. Karila and Alasuutari, 2012) (see also Chapter 7). Besides, children's perspectives and position can be fairly weak in the IDP process in preschools (cf. Alasuutari & Karila, 2010; Vallberg-Roth, 2010). IDPs seem to rely largely on the tradition of observing children and doing developmental psychological assessments (Alasuutari & Karila, 2010; Elfström, 2004; Lenz-Taguchi, 2000; Lutz, 2009; Nordin-Hultman, 2004; Palla, 2011; Vallberg-Roth & Månsson, 2006, 2008, 2009).

Vallberg-Roth and Månsson (2006) argue that IDPs can be seen and termed as *normal plans* rather than as individual plans (cf. Chapter 6). The normal plan reflects the standard of normality against which children are measured. This standard is characterized partly by stage theories of developmental psychology, with their universal claims, and partly by the expression of a monolingual norm. The normal plan also encompasses templates with a relatively locked-in structure based on established 'normal' knowledge stages/goals in relation to defined subjects.

The normal plan can, rather, be characterized as individually oriented instead of individual. It concentrates on the individual insofar as a plan (or template/form) is developed (or completed) for each child. Further, there appears to be some leeway here for the individual to climb the ladder of needs, formulate personal goals, and decide how (and how quickly) goals and activities are to be accomplished. However, the plans cannot be considered individual in the sense that they are personally designed or inter-culturally adapted; consequently, the term individually oriented normal plans is considered a more precise designation of the phenomenon in practice than individual development plans (Vallberg-Roth & Månsson, 2006).

The documentation tools described above stress democratic ideals with participation as a mode that promotes motivation. The presented forms of documentation are fairly open, with emphasis on (unstructured) observation and vague assessment criteria, although the cultural discourses and conventions are intertwined. However, more standardized practices of documentation are also part of present-day ECE; we consider these next.

Standardized documents – TRAS, Second Step and START

As an example of standardized documentation tools, we will first look at *TRAS*, a Norwegian observational material. Theoretically, it is founded on developmental psychology and linguistics. It can be described as an interprofessional co-production, since it was created by speech therapists, psychologists, special education teachers, linguists and preschool teachers.

TRAS builds on assumptions about the age-dependency of children's skills. The material addresses three main areas: interaction and attention; language comprehension and awareness; and pronunciation, word production and sentence structure. The child's skills and competences are recorded in a schedule consisting of age-specific statements and questions. For example, the following questions are presented regarding the language development of four- to five-year-olds:

Can the child tell riddles/jokes?

Can the child write his/her name?

Can the child pronounce the 's' sound correctly?

Does the child use because sentences?

(Espenakk, 2003, pp. 2–3)

The teacher will then assess and record the degree to which the child masters each skill in one of three categories: has not mastered, partially mastered, or mastered. The teacher is also advised to check that the child understands the assignments, and to systemically search for areas where the child lacks words or has little understanding (Wagner & Kari, 2004).

Bugge (2010) and Johansen-Lyngseth (2010) argue for the benefits of TRAS observations in preschools. According to Bugge (2010), systematic analysis with TRAS gives clear evidence of children's linguistic development. Furthermore, the need for support, if present, becomes apparent, and teachers are provided with an opportunity for reflection and a basis for conversations with parents.

Østrem (2010) also considers the TRAS observation material but addresses how detailed objectives formulated in the material steer early education away from its basic values. Østrem notes that the Norwegian preschool is based on democratic values that underline fulfilling children's needs for care, play and versatile learning. She underscores that the approach to learning expressed through detailed objectives and analysis of children's language development is not completely compatible with the core standards and values of the Norwegian national curriculum (cf. Pettersvold & Østrem, 2012).

Another standardized material used in the preschools of our case example is the *Second Step* (Löwenborg & Gislason, 2010a), a life skills programme developed in the USA for ECE that claims to be evidence-based (see www.cfchildren.org). The primary aim of the programme is to support children's development into socially- and emotionally-skilled individuals. The Second Step programme includes three main areas: empathy training; impulse control and problem solving; and self-control. Documentation and assessment is done through the forms of logbooks, evaluations and information letters which can either focus on children or educators or be addressed to parents. The teaching programme is based on age norms derived from developmental psychology, and its objectives are formulated in terms of knowledge that children should have as well as goals they should achieve:

> The objectives for learning in Second Step with respect to empathy are that children will have the ability to: Read emotions by perceiving signs (facial expression, body language) and situation-specific signals (context). /.../ Understand that people may have different feelings for the same thing. /.../ Anticipate feelings. /.../ Distinguish between intentional acts and accidents.
>
> *(Löwenborg & Gislason, 2010a, pp. 35–6)*

The Second Step programme is aimed at children aged 4–6. The social and emotional learning programme *START* is similar to it but addresses children aged 1–3 (Löwenborg & Gislason, 2010b). START has been developed in Sweden and translated into Danish and Norwegian, and it focuses on three main areas. The first concerns the child's ability to recognize and name six basic emotions: joy, sadness, anger, fear, surprise/amazement and distaste/disgust. The second area is called connection and affinity, and the third area includes training and understanding of some basic interaction skills, such as taking turns and waiting. The intervention programme is theoretically grounded in psychology and structured around exercises with different themes. The exercises are introduced to groups of children and serve as a basis for intervention in all everyday situations in ECE. The work is documented by using a standardized log consisting of eighteen different categories; 'the log section is an aid for teachers to know what was addressed, how much progress was made, to ensure that all children were involved and an evaluating follow-up in everyday life' (p. 5). As with Second Step, the START programme also involves parents as partners, so that the various skills can be reinforced both at preschool and at home: 'Parents can also get the material themselves if they should wish to do so' (p. 19). The creators of the published programme are both psychologists.

The standardized tools of documentation, like the ones presented above, are explicitly concerned with assessment. As assessment tools, they can look easier to comprehend than the more open means of documentation. However, we can still develop further the conceptual examination of both of these types of documentation and consider what forms of assessment are deployed with them.

Different forms of assessment

Formative assessment and summative assessment are concepts that often appear in educational literature when the appraisal of knowledge and education are discussed (e.g. Black & Wiliam, 2009, Buldu, 2010; Harrison & Howard, 2009; Lindström, Lindberg & Pettersson, 2011; Taras, 2009). *Formative assessment* can be described as a valuation of what happens during the learning process. It is forward-looking and aims to support the student's continued learning and development. Formative assessment underscores feedback to the students and their active participation in the assessment process. For instance, the IDPs in Swedish schools must have a formative function; they should emphasize the students' developmental opportunities and support the students' continued learning (Skolverket, 2008b).

In ECE, pedagogical documentation, IDPs, the portfolio and learning stories can be linked with formative assessment (e.g. Buldu, 2010; Carr & Lee, 2012; Lindström et al., 2011). For example, Black and Wiliam assert the following:

> The term 'assessment' refers to all those activities undertaken by teachers, and by their students in assessing themselves, which provide information to be used as feedback to modify the teaching and learning activities in which they

are engaged. Such assessment becomes 'formative assessment' when the evidence is actually used to adapt the teaching work to meet the needs.

(Black & Wiliam, 1998, p. 2)

Summative assessment refers to a valuation of what children have ultimately learned at the end of an activity, instruction period or theme/project. Hence, it looks backwards. Often, it is also based on various assessment data. Grades are a typical example of summative assessment. As will be shown later in this chapter, grade-like assessment of knowledge has also become evident in the Nordic ECE. Sometimes summative assessment is described as an assessment *of* learning as opposed to formative assessment that is characterized as an assessment *for* learning (Vallberg-Roth, 2012b).

The research literature on formative and summative assessments is contradictory. There are studies which argue for formative assessment and suggest that it helps children to perceive what is considered to be valuable and what is considered as knowledge in different subjects (e.g. Lindberg, 2005). However, the definition of formative assessment is also criticized for being too broad and imprecise (Bennet, 2011). Moreover, some suggest that all assessment can be viewed as essentially summative; there is no purely formative assessment (see Taras, 2009). Others argue that summative and formative assessment may be viewed as complementary (e.g. Giota, 2006). Research also shows that summative and formative assessment can coexist in documentation at the individual level (IDP) (Vallberg-Roth, 2009).

However, there is a variety of assessment forms used in ECE that cannot be completely reduced to formative or summative assessments. The concepts of developmental-psychological assessment, knowledge assessment, personal assessment, self-assessment, and narrative assessment, as well as assessment focusing on the performance of the centre, are more apt in characterizing many of the assessment forms.

Developmental-psychological assessments are based on assumptions that a child's skills in areas such as language, motor skills and social-emotional development are age-specific, as in the following examples:

1–3 years: Children notice that other children are larger or smaller than themselves. Children begin to respond empathically – for example, by giving a doll to someone who is sad (Löwenborg & Gislason, 2010b, p. 34).

2–3 years: Children begin to name different phenomena and talk to themselves about what they are doing (Löwenborg & Gislason, 2010b, p. 43).

2–3 years: Can the child pronounce words with m, n, and p, b, t, d? (For example man, nose, papa, car, tent, damp?) (Espenakk, 2003, p. 3).

As was previously mentioned, the tradition of observing children and assessing their psychological development is evident not only in the standardized tools (e.g. TRAS and Second Step) but also in more open means of documentation, such as

IDPs (Alasuutari & Karila, 2010; Elfström, 2004; Lenz-Taguchi, 2000; Lutz, 2009; Nordin-Hultman, 2004; Vallberg-Roth & Månsson, 2006, 2008). The purpose is to assess children's development in relation to already predetermined categories which define what a normal child should be able to do at a particular age.[8] These assessments of psychological development can merge with knowledge assessments.

In *knowledge assessments*, the child's learning may also be graded. Preschool teachers can record, among other factors, when the child reaches different stages or learning outcomes according to predetermined categories such as 'never, sometimes and for the most part' or 'able to, partially able to, or not able to'. Below, is an example of this:

> Speaks clearly with all speech sounds and correct word order
>
> Names at least fifteen letters
>
> Writes name in correct writing direction
>
> Recites numbers by rote
>
> *(Vallberg-Roth & Månsson, 2008, pp. 31–2)*

In the above example, the knowledge assessments resemble grades. They assess the degree to which knowledge objectives in language and mathematics are achieved for young children. Hence, they can be interpreted as a form of summative assessment.[9] They can be seen as contradictory to the general approach of the Nordic ECE systems that usually avoid exact assessment of children.

The documentation can also include *personal assessments*, which are common in child portfolios and in IDPs. The judgments about the child's personality are usually positive, but they can also be negative and critical:

> Charming, intelligent, fun
>
> Alert, resourceful, plays well
>
> She can be scattered and distracted
>
> Can easily flip out and not care
>
> He is peaceful and harmonious

Personality assessments as an aspect of systematic documentation are an important issue to address and discuss. For example, the Swedish National Agency for Education (Skolverket, 2008a, 2008b) states that the individual development plan should not include scores of students' personal qualities and that the teacher should use objective language. Despite this, personality assessments are a phenomenon of IDPs and individual development conferences (see Chapter 7), by which, for example, parents can be encouraged to assess their children by using the so-called 'Strengths Cards' (Markström, 2010, 2011a). The cards have adjectives printed on them – 'determined', 'energetic', 'adaptable', 'independent' – that can be perceived either positively or negatively. Teachers contend that these cards are a method of engaging parents in the conferences. Markström (2011a) proposes that the use of the cards can serve as a method for teachers to distance themselves and leave the categorization to the parents.

Self-assessments can be related to formative assessments and meta-cognitive theory, which underlines the ability of the individuals to consider and assess their own learning. This kind of assessment may appear in the portfolios and interviews with children (see Chapter 5), such as 'I thought this was fun, difficult, boring; I have learned this; I want to learn that'. The following text was written in one of the portfolios analysed in our study:

> What do you usually do at preschool?
>
> Eating food and are out playing, painting a pattern.
>
> What do you think is the most fun to do at preschool?
>
> Playing with stuff and go home. Fun drawing in preschool.
>
> Is there anything that you find difficult?
>
> Draw text.
>
> What are you good at?
>
> Drawing dragons and dinosaurs.
>
> What would you like to improve?
>
> Become bigger and marry mom and dad and Mia.
>
> What do you want to learn?
>
> Draw text.
>
> How will you learn it?
>
> I'm getting bigger.
>
> What do you like about yourself?
>
> Happy with my little sister.

In the key competences for lifelong learning, the EU also underlines learning to assess one's strengths and weaknesses, as is done in portfolios and learning stories. Regarding entrepreneurship, it states the following:

> Skills relate to proactive project management (involving, for example the ability to plan, organise, manage, lead and delegate, analyse, communicate, de-brief, evaluate and record), effective representation and negotiation, and the ability to work both as an individual and collaboratively in teams. The ability to judge and identify one's strengths and weaknesses, and to assess and take risks as and when warranted, is essential.
>
> *(European Communities, 2007, p. 11)*

Entrepreneurship and entrepreneurial learning comprise a market-oriented (educational) content that can be interpreted as strengthening a goal- and result-oriented management system (cf. Andersen-Østergaard, Hjort & Skytthe-Kaarsberg-Schmidt, 2008). The background to the EU's key competences is said to be 'that as globalization continues to confront the European Union with new challenges, each citizen will need a wide range of key competences to adapt flexibly to a rapidly changing and highly interconnected world' (European Community, 2007, p. 2). The individual-oriented target structure in the form of key competences is also orienting the focus of assessment and evaluation on the individual, which may be problematic in relation to the definition of goals in the Nordic ECE curricula. Similarly, intensified self-assessment, self-reflection and self-regulation can be interpreted as manifestations of a global society and a reflexive modernization, a process of modernization that is characteristic of risk society (e.g. Beck, 1992; Foucault, 2008; Giddens, 1997).

Systematic documentation and children's self-assessments can also be considered in the view of neuroscientific research, which suggests that the area in the frontal lobe, the decision-making centre of the brain, develops late and is not mature until after age 20 (Giedd, 2007). Consequently, children and young people may not yet have developed abilities such as impulse control, gaining an overview, planning for the future, sifting through impressions and assessing risk. Hence, it seems that children are exposed to documentation and (self-) assessment long before they develop the abilities required for them. Therefore, the neuroscientific research encourages us to question whether it is desirable to work with self-assessment and standardized programmes on impulse control for children in preschool.

Many of the assessment tools also deploy *narrative assessment*. In portfolios, telling stories of learning, reflecting on the past, and, sometimes, planning for the future can involve both adults and children. They can also take place as a boundary object that connects ECE and home. Carr and Lee (2012) point out that learning stories take a credit rather than a deficit approach to assessment; they argue that the outcomes in early education are learning dispositions and learner identities. In narrative assessments as boundary objects, one can see how people acquire values and views from those around them, and, therefore, the assessment is 'overtaken' (cf. Latour, 2005, 'Action is overtaken'), mixed and transformed. The voice and activity of the child is often constructed – mainly by the adults – into a joint story. Even though the child may be involved in the documentation process, she or he might not fully understand its consequences (see also Chapter 5).

In the following example, the learning story includes the child's, teacher's and parent's views, and comprises a mix of self and personal assessments:

> Peaceful and harmonious boy. Mom says I can be anything but calm at times. Have your own will and wish happy that it is followed but I'm easy to persuade. I go to swimming lessons, and soon I'll start playing football. /.../ Likes to play games with mom and wrestling with Dad and watch TV. /.../ Think it's super fun to talk, talk, and talk.

Narrative assessment can also be woven into the documentation practice without being noted and or problematized. This can be illustrated by an excerpt taken from the guidelines for pedagogical documentation by the National Agency for Education in Sweden (Skolverket, 2012). While it is the relational and the materiality as agents that are highlighted in the agency's guidelines, it is the individual's skills and knowledge that seem to be the target of assessment:

> If we compare the first opportunity with the other, we can also in this summary report clearly see that the children were not 'clay-exploring' children in the first sequence, although one of the children says she loves clay, but quickly became different in themselves – became 'clay-explorers' – when the activity changed on the second occasion.
>
> *(Skolverket, 2012, p. 38)*

According to the guidelines, pedagogical documentation focuses on the child as becoming different in herself or himself, mentioned as consistent with the policy (Skolverket, 2012). The pedagogical documentation is intended to follow the child's development, and the child should be compared only to itself. However, it is obvious that the desired child is, for example, a child defined as a clay-exploring child, in other words, a performing and active problem-solving child (cf. Popkewitz, 2008). The children are not only compared to themselves; they are assessed against a (non-established) norm in the example of a clay-exploring individual (cf. Alasuutari & Markström, 2011; Vallberg-Roth, 2011). It can be asked whether it is primarily the child related to the material and a scientific rational understanding of the world which is enhanced. If this is the case, the child as an exploring researcher can be seen as the desirable child in pedagogical documentation.

The next quotation from the Swedish guidelines (Skolverket, 2012) shows even more clearly that even if it is the relational that is focused on, it is not the relation(al) that learn and is assessed (cf. Biesta, 2011). It is the child's sign of learning, performance and competence that is valued and assessed. In the quotation, the preschool teacher, or *co-researcher*, is assessing the character of child's knowledge and exploration depicted as an on-going condition of the child becoming different in itself:

> Now he knows he can. Now he owns the technology.
>
> *(Skolverket, 2012, p. 50)*

Finally, there are also examples of assessment that focus on the ECE centre: they examine how specific activities affect children and how the activities or their environment can be changed to support the children in their learning and development (cf. Vallberg-Roth, 2011a). The *centre-focused assessment* is based on socio-cultural and context-oriented approaches. In the following instructions concerning pedagogical documentation, the assessment of the centre and the educational environment is intertwined with the assessment of the individual child:

Reggio Emilia inspired individual development plan

Describe, explain and SHOW, supported by the documentation, what the child is doing and is interested in right now: Here we talk about documentation, images, video, audio, that demonstrate the interests we see in the child. We look at situations where children are creative, amazed, where they will find their place and are able to express themselves.

Describe how the above issues can be deepened, challenged and developed: We reflect on how we could develop these situations and challenges for the children. What would we wish that the child could encounter, what we would like to offer and how can we challenge the child? How will the children have the opportunity to grow?

Based on the above, describe concrete changes to the activity: We reflect on how we can change for the child to find those opportunities. What can we specifically offer children, what situations can we invite them to explore? What does the child need in terms of materials, time, situation, group, etc.?

(Vallberg- Roth, 2011b, pp. 155–6)

The assessment in the above example focuses on the child's interests and issues as well as the challenges, teacher support, and learning environment that the child needs. The focus then turns into what is important to offer the child in terms of content, materials, space, time, groups, relations, actions and communication.

Concluding discussion

The three preschools in the case study described in this chapter worked with between six to ten different documentation forms, including pedagogical documentation, portfolios, learning stories, individual development plans, parent questionnaires, evidence-related and standardized documents (such as TRAS, SET, START), and Second Step. Electronic documentation was also found. The documentation tools varied between fairly open and largely standardized documents. In all, the practices of the three preschools exemplify the wide-ranging and extensive nature of documentation in the activities that take place in the ECE institutions. We call this phenomenon *multi-documentation* (also Vallberg-Roth, 2012b).

Multi-documentation comprises of a variety of assessment forms that cannot be completely or easily reduced to formative or summative assessments. Instead, the documentation practices provide a sample of developmental-psychological assessments, knowledge assessments (sometimes graded), personal assessments, self-assessments, narrative assessments, centre-performance-focused assessments and activity-oriented assessment.

The majority of documentation tools stress democratic ideals with participation as a mode that promotes motivation. According to teachers, documentation can highlight and increase awareness and an understanding of the development, abilities and skills of the individual child, as well as processes in the group and the learning environment. With the support of documentation, children and adults describe, explain and show the child's actions, interests and questions. Moreover, preschool teachers argue that, for example, portfolios can show children their learning in the course of time and provide them something to display, revisit and be proud of. Meta-cognitive learning in children (their knowledge of their own learning) is then highlighted. Documentation can be used to support children in need of special support as well as children in need of more challenges. Moreover, documentation can be used to provide parents with greater insight, improve the quality of peda-gogical work, and clearly monitor and have evidence of what is happening (cf. Vallberg-Roth, 2012b).

In a critical view, the systematic documentation may be seen as a tool to gov-ern the individual child to actively take responsibility for their own learning and for assessing their own efforts. It requires a high degree of self-reflection, meaning that children are expected to inform about their deliberations, internal sensations, feelings and things they can improve on. Even when it is underscored that the activities of ECE are being assessed (rather than the children), often the opposite seems to occur. The children's personal qualities, skills and abilities are observed and assessed, and the measures taken are often directed at the individual child. However, there are also examples in which the observation focuses more on the process and what the teacher offers in learning situations. In these cases, the assess-ment can concern the specific content of education – concrete situations, signs of learning processes and the environment – with the aim of providing the child with the opportunities needed to develop and learn.

Generally, we can ask if it is even possible to document learning (cf. Biesta, 2011; Andersen-Østergaard et al., 2008). One could argue that learning and learning processes are inaccessible (i.e., not possible to observe) and intangible (i.e., ideas, smells and tastes); using this perspective, learning cannot be recorded. Various forms of documentation are based on recording what is interpreted as signs of learning, and there is then an extensive variety of interpretive possi-bilities. The observer transforms and constructs the meaning of the registered subject/object; hence, documentation serves as a surface on which the adult projects her or his notions. It is also argued that registration (documentation) makes much of the context invisible and reduces the individual and actor (Andersen-Østergaard et al., 2008).

Our examination shows that the different forms of documentation all have double edges. On the one hand, they can give means to empower, support and strengthen children, professionals and parents. This is also how documentation practices are typically described in literature on early education; they are ascribed primarily positive, democratic and emancipatory potentials (Vallberg-Roth, 2010). On the other hand, the documentation practices also have their limitations. It is important to examine and consider if and how they can also weaken, mislead and restrict children, parents and professionals both in research and in practice. Additionally, more attention should be paid to the question of whether children grow up in an atmosphere where it is not possible for them to politely decline documentation concerning them. Are they made to believe in the importance of constant self-assessments, confessions about their inner feelings, and the need to show what you can master in the name of sustainable lifelong learning? Instead, perhaps we should consider how children would be supported by establishing a curious and critical stance regarding systematic documentation.

Notes

1   SET is a social and emotional training programme for children in ECE constructed by Birgitta Kimber and Carina Petré (2009). The programme is based on developmental psychology and prescribes goals about children's ability to recognize, name and handle their basic feelings. These are documented in SET-books or portfolios (see also Kimber, 2011). The programme also involves parents as partners so that the various skills can be reinforced both at preschool and at home.
2   Second Step is a life skills programme for ECE and school that claims to be evidence-based. The programme has been developed in the USA and it is used in many countries. See:

> *Second Step* – USA, Canada (www.cfchildren.org)
> *Trin for Trin* – Denmark (www.cesel.dk)
> *Second Step* – England (www.secondstep.org.uk)
> *Askeleittain* – Finland (www.askeleittain.fi)
> *Faustlos* – Germany (www.faustlos.de)
> *Tulleriit* – Greenland (www.inerisaavik.gl)
> *Segundo Paso* – Guatemala, Venezuela, El Salvador (www.seccatid.gob.gt)
> *Hengaw be Hengaw* – Kurdistan, Iraq (www.komak.nu)
> *Stig af stigi* – Iceland (www.reynismenn.is)
> *Sekando Suteppo* – Japan (www.cfc-j.org)
> *Žingsnis po žingsnio* – Lithuania (www.pvc.lt)
> *Steg for steg* – Norway (www.prososial.no)
> *Srdce Na Dlani* – Slovakia (www.fphil.uniba.sk)
> *StegVis* – Sweden (www.gislasonlowenborg.com)

3   RUS (Relationship Development Scheme) is structured around four areas: (1) Relationship to educators; (2) Safe in the environment; (3) Relation to peers; and (4) Term the world (children's linguistic development). The teacher documents these areas in a logbook (see Sundblad, 2006).
4   Step sheets measure different fields of knowledge and include about 200 objects of knowledge concerning language, mathematics, science and motor skills.
5   START ('Life Skills for the Youngest') (Löwenborg & Gislason, 2010b) is a social and emotional learning programme for the use of professionals who work with children aged 1–3 years. It has been developed in Sweden.
6   TRAS is a standardized Norwegian observational material about language, also used in Sweden and Denmark. Theoretically, it is based on developmental psychology and linguistics.
7   There are two other concepts that are close to the IDP but have a different meaning: an individual educational plan and an individualized educational programme (both abbreviated with IEP). In international literature these two concepts refer usually to a practice of special education: a child with special needs is provided with an IEP (e.g. Drasgow, Yell & Robinson, 2001; Etscheidt, 2006). However, in Finnish ECE individual educational plans are drafted for all children. Thus, in Finland the IEPs are used very much in a similar manner as the IDPs in Sweden. Only the Finnish regulations are contradictory to the Swedish one: IEPs are required in ECE but not in primary education.

8   The expectations of what is normal at different ages are, however, culture bound. Notions of the age when children are assumed to be toilet-trained comprise one example of cultural variation (e.g.Vandenbroeck, Boonaert, van Der Mespel & de Brabaundere, 2009).

9   This kind of assessment is incompatible with the Swedish national curriculum and policy (Vallberg-Roth, 2009, 2010; Vallberg-Roth & Månsson, 2011). The Education Act (*Ds 2009: 25*) states that preschool children should neither be assessed based on established standards nor be compared to anyone but themselves. However, predefined standards are used in both the age-normed assessments based on developmental psychology and in the graded knowledge assessments.

4

TEACHERS IN INTENSIFIED ASSESSMENT AND DOCUMENTATION PRACTICES

A didaktik approach

Assessment has often been discussed from the perspective of didactics, that is, from the Anglo-Saxon tradition that tends to focus on methods, instructions and learning outcomes (cf. Bennett, 2010; Gundem & Hopmann, 1998; OECD, 2012). In this chapter, we employ a different view of assessment: We consider assessment and documentation practices in early childhood education (ECE) from the perspective of didaktik, and, thus, we develop the concept of transformative assessment and consider the teacher's role in it.[1] Didaktik refers to a Continental (European) approach that emphasizes the reflective processes of 'Bildung'.[2] The didaktik approach allows teachers to critically consider the intertwining between assessment and documentation. A critical reflection considers the content, the form, the function, and the actor of the assessment as an integrated whole (Uljens, 1997, 2006). Documents are then seen as co-actors in educational processes. To mark the difference from Anglo-Saxon didactics, the Continental approach is written with the letter k, *didaktik*.

Three types of questions are consequential to the didaktik approach in documentation and assessment practices: *What, how* and *why* to document and assess (Gundem, 1997; Lindberg, 2011; Uljens, 1997). Of these questions, *why* is the most foundational one since it concerns the function, purpose and legitimacy of assessments and documentation.

Another didaktik question is what should be assessed – the object as content. Is the focus on the punctual results, the products or the processes? Attention may also be placed on personal characteristics and developmental psychological stages, or on values, imagination and critical skills. *How* relates to how the assessment is performed: What kinds of documentation and what forms of assessment are used? These questions have already been addressed in the previous chapter.

In addition, *who, when* and *where* are other questions that may be incorporated in didaktik. Who should assess whom and for whom? Should children assess themselves and one another, or should they be assessed by teachers, managers, inspectors and parents? The teachers may also assess themselves or may be assessed by children, parents or inspectors. Further, we should consider where and when the assessment takes place: Should it be implemented at different age-levels and in different locations, at the ECE centre or at home, inside or outside, and before, during or after activities?

Thus, the didaktik approach provides a lengthy list of questions to reflect on. In this chapter, not only will we apply the *why* question as our primary tool, but also we will build our discussion on our findings from the previous chapter, which concerned the content and different forms of assessment in ECE (the examination of 'what' and 'how' questions). The *why* question deals with the function of documentation and assessment and requires us to consider their justification. When considering this, we will use Biesta's (2011) definitions of the qualification, socialization or subjectification functions as our frames of reference. Through examining the didaktik questions, we will develop and discuss the tentative concept of *transformative assessment* in *multi-documentation*. Transformative assessment (Vallberg-Roth, 2011b; Vallberg-Roth & Månsson, 2008) is a concept that captures the complex assessment and documentation practices that appear in our empirical material. Furthermore, it provides a new perspective on the role of the teacher as a *trans-actor* in multi-documentation.

Our discussion will again draw on the empirical data from the three preschools analysed in the previous chapter: the centre with a Reggio Emilia profile; the preschool that underlines the view of children as unique individuals; and the setting with a health profile. We will apply both documentary data and teacher interviews from these preschools.

As shown in the previous chapter, the documentation practices of the three preschools varied, as often seems to be the case more generally. In the preschool with a Reggio Emilia profile, pedagogical documentation was underlined. The preschool emphasizing the uniqueness of children applied individual developmental plans, a teacher folder and a child portfolio. Finally, the preschool with a health profile worked also primarily with portfolios. Generally, each of the preschools focused on children's social development and language competence. Hence, these would be the main answers to the didaktik question of what is being assessed. The three preschools deployed partly overlapping and partly different forms of assessment, including knowledge assessment, narrative assessment and self-assessment. Thus, they gave multiple answers to the didaktik question *how*. Finally, we could identify children as the answer to the question of who is being assessed. Children were the predominant targets of documentation in the three preschools. It is now important to consider what seems to be the more general purpose of documentation and assessment in these settings.

Why – the function of the documentation and assessment

Education is a composite concept, and this becomes apparent when considering its purpose. Biesta (2009, 2011) argues that both researchers and educators should further investigate and discuss the purpose and functions of education. He suggests that education serves (at least) three different functions: *qualification*, *socialization* and *subjectification*.

The function of qualification concerns ways in which education contributes to the acquisition of knowledge, skills and dispositions that qualify one to do something. In this context, to qualify means to equip individuals with the knowledge for citizenship, cultural understanding and working life.

The second function of education concerns ways in which individuals become part of existing socio-cultural orders; this is the socialization function of education. Through socialization – that is, the transmission of norms and values – the education incorporates the individual into the social order. The individual is inserted into the existing ways of doing and being (see Chapters 5 and 7) in relation to other factors, including others, oneself, work and learning (cf. Popkewitz, 2008).

Finally, the third function, subjectification, concerns ways in which education contributes to individual freedom, personal voice and uniqueness. It can be understood as the opposite of socialization. Socialization relates to how we are part of a large, comprehensive order, and uniqueness expresses how we differ from this order. Subjectification refers to how the individual initiates an action, a beginning, but is also subjected to its consequences through how others perceive and assess her/his beginnings and actions.

The functions of qualification, socialization and subjectification that are presented by Biesta (2011) are neither separate nor totally overlapping, but interwoven and related to one another. They can be identified also in the ECE documentation, as will be shown next through our case study example.

The functions of documentation in the three preschools

All three functions of documentation – subjectification, qualification and socialization – can be identified in the documentation practices of the three preschools in our case study. However, the emphasis of the functions varies between the documentation practices in the preschools.

The function of subjectification – hence, the focus on the individual in relations – is most salient in the pedagogical documentation of the Reggio Emilia-inspired preschool, but mainly in interplay with socialising and qualifying functions. It can be identified, for example, in the documentation of activities that concentrate on creative work with different materials in small groups. In the following, a teacher explains her remarks regarding a situation in which the children have been provided with clay and the opportunity to study it/play with it in relation to an overhead projector (the glass on the overhead projector is covered with clay):

TEACHER: He did not touch the clay; he was only interested in the light. How should we interpret this? Well, this boy is very interested in plugs, sockets and light. Then you need to find the niche of how we will challenge him? /.../ Then we have the girl who sat next to him; she just wanted to build with the clay. She was not so interested in the light itself, but she wanted to build with clay next to him on the table. How are we going to challenge her next time?

The teacher discusses the differences in the focus of two children in the situation and notes their respective actions with the available material. She interprets and assesses the children's actions and initiatives as differing interests that will require individual challenges next time.

The subjectification function is also evident in the documentation practices of the other two preschools. In the preschool emphasizing children as unique individuals, it can be identified especially in pedagogical documentation. In the preschool with a health profile, the subjectification function is evidenced in portfolios. The following excerpts show this function in the documentation concerning language, drawing and self-portraits in the portfolio:

TEACHER 1: And we write exactly as the children say; we will not change anything. So, sometimes the sentences seem very strange, but it is exactly as the children say. /.../ And it's very important that we respect the children; it is their portfolio.

TEACHER 2: When we have suggested that the children draw a self portrait, some have been unwilling. No, they wanted to draw a fish or a dinosaur. /.../ So, you do not need be locked in to your ideas for it is possible that they may not want to do self-portraits.

The qualification function, which refers to concentrating on the acquisition of knowledge, skills and competence, is most clearly shown in the documentation from the preschool that emphasizes its view of children as unique individuals. For example, the preschool deploys the Step sheets as a detailed guideline to document children's development and competence in several areas such as communication, mathematics and science. The qualification function is also shown in the documents from the preschool with the health profile. At this preschool, the children's portfolios may include assessments on their language development (TRAS) and documentation on their skills in mathematical thinking. Lastly, the qualification function is also evident in the Reggio Emilia-profiled preschool's documentation of language development, as shown in the following interview answer by a teacher:

TEACHER: What words does this child master? Can the child master any words at all? Especially here in this area, we have a high degree of immigrants. We have lots of parents and children – they can't speak Swedish, but they can do other things. But we need to be alert, to check.

Finally, we have the socialization function, which seems to be most evident in the documents from the preschool with the health profile. For instance, life skills and social development are highlighted in the documentation of, for example, START and Second Step (see Chapter 3), in documentation about 'friend projects' and in portfolios with themes concerning social development. Social behaviours, such as learning to wait, to take turns, and to be a good friend, are also emphasized in the teacher interviews as the basic values of the preschool:

TEACHER: Then you had photographed this (friend-project addressing social values) too, and these are the very basic values of our education work. /.../ The fact is that we have many small children, and everyone is supposed to be nice to each other, but they are not always. So, we need to work with values all the time. You can see the progress when they start school; it's a tough climate. So, it's really important that we work with it, and this was so tangible. I thought it was a good way to demonstrate and show the children – especially when they sat in these different groups. And you can see it documented also in the photo and photo frames, and you can see what has happened and what we have done.

The socialization function can also be identified in the documentation of the two other preschools. In the preschool with a Reggio Emilia profile, the socio-emotional development is in focus, for example, through the use of Second Step and in its assessments about apologising, being a good friend and taking turns (see Chapter 3). In the preschool that underlines children as unique individuals, the socialization function is salient, for example, in the use of Relation Development Schemes.

Thus, the emphases of the three functions of education vary in the documentation practices of the three preschools. This variation is linked with the documentation and assessment tools that are applied in the respective settings. Hence, the case study illuminates how decisions regarding documentation are, more generally, consequential. It can even be asked whether the variation can eventually lead to different outcomes and orientations for children depending on, for example, where they grow up and attend preschool (cf. Chapter 6). Additionally, the variation gives another picture regarding the complexities of documentation and assessment in ECE.

Transformative assessment

In Chapter 3, we illustrated the multi-documentation in Nordic ECE that entails the teachers' switching between different forms of documentation and assessment. Above, we described how this multi-documentation constitutes and constructs the interplay between different functions of education, even though it can also orientate to a specific educational purpose, such as socialization. Consequently, we argue that the assessment intertwined in multi-documentation and potentially betokening multiple purposes cannot be thoroughly captured either with the traditionally well-known concepts of summative and formative assessment or with any of the individual forms of assessment discussed thus far. Instead, the concept of *transformative assessment* is more suitable when considering assessment in ECE (Vallberg-Roth, 2012b).

Transformative assessment is a concept that can be related to the didaktik questions *what*, *who*, *how* and *why* (Vallberg-Roth, 2012b). It can also be regarded as interplay between linear (goal-directed) and non-linear (rhizomatic) assessment, and between punctual (summative) and processual (formative) assessment. The transformative nature of assessment becomes also salient in our interviews with teachers. In the following extended quotation, a preschool teacher describes documentation and assessment practices in her preschool:

TEACHER: One can say that there are quite a number of different types of documentation. /…/ I need to be observant. What words does this child master? Can the child master any words at all? Especially in this area we have a high degree of immigrants. We have lots of parents and children – they can't speak Swedish but they can do other things. But we need to be alert, to check. It will be a little different than, now I have frozen ice cubes. And I have coloured them red with food colouring and put them in a large bowl and put it on the floor. And now, we let in the four yearlings. Now I will just watch and see what happens here. So, that is a different type of documentation; it is not more or less important.

In the beginning of the quote, the teacher notes the general need to be alert in her position, hence, to observe. The observation can centre on an individual child, for example, on how many words a particular child masters. In this, the teacher is discussing assessment that can be characterized as goal-directed, punctual or summative assessment. When the teacher describes the ice-cube setting provided for the four yearlings, she is constructing a rhizomatic situation with non-linear and processual assessment, but in this case regarding activity at the group-level.

The concept of transformative assessment can express practices between different levels. It is not concerned only with the shifting focus between an individual and group activity, as in the previous example, but it can also include the institutional and societal level, as well as offline and online assessment. Transformative assessment can thus include a community-oriented approach in addition to involving preschool activities. It can be defined as a boundary object (cf. Star & Griesemer, 1989) at the micro (individual and group activity level), meso (between institutions and different service provisions, etc.) and macro level (state government, science, market and civil spheres). With objects we mean social objects as acts (cf. Ferraris, 2013). However, the boundaries at and between different levels are perforated and porous: they are neither totally separated nor fully overlapping. Therefore, assessment in documentation also moves across these boundaries.

Transformative assessment as a boundary object at the micro-level

At the micro level in our data, the concept of transformative assessment can articulate and conceptually capture the interaction between different functions, forms and actors of documentation and assessment. For example, the qualification, socialization and subjectification functions can be interwoven with and related to one another in a transforming interplay. The assessments may also move between an individual and the activity of the group. Different tools of assessment and documentation may transcend the perforated boundaries between personal-, self-, developmental and knowledge assessments, such as in IDPs and portfolios. This is illustrated in the following example from a portfolio:

> During the theme, we talked about the size, appearance, differences and similarities between different trees, looked up different trees and talked even more. We have expanded our vocabulary and practiced our conceptualisation of the tree as a base. /.../ In the photo, Ben made pear prints in various colours as pasted up on the magic tree. /.../ Ben made two trees: one large and one small. I'm in the photograph, and I have two sticks in my hand: a short one and a long one.

In this example, the documentation and assessment move between group level ('we have') and individual level ('Ben made'), knowledge assessment (the size of 'our vocabulary') and self-assessment ('I'm in the photograph, and I have two sticks in my hand: a short one and a long one'), teacher and child as subjects, and between text and photograph.

The assessment can also be transformed from feedback at the individual level to feed forward at the preschool-activity level. Hence, the backward- and current-looking assessment at the individual level can be transformed into the forward-looking assessment at the level of preschool activity. The assessment moves then from systematic documentation monitoring signs of child development and learning at the individual level – for example, in language – to an assessment of the preschool activity: that which needs to be changed in order for the child to further develop in line with curriculum goals (Vallberg-Roth, 2012b).

Thus, transformative assessment is not based on feedback or feed forward in relation to fixed and predetermined knowledge requirements or goals to achieve for the individual, which is the case in summative and formative assessment (see Chapter 3). Even though summative and formative assessments also focus on how the student develops understanding, self-assessment and peer-assessment and considers teaching in the classroom, they do not conceptualize assessment as a phenomenon at the boundary between school, home and other institutions as the notion of transformative assessment does.

Transformative assessment as a boundary object at the meso level

As has been discussed in previous chapters, many of the documentation tools involve not only teachers and children but also parents and sometimes other professionals. This is often the case with portfolios, learning stories, individual educational plans (IEPs), and health and development registration. The communication and collaborative documentation practices between different actors are one example of transformative assessment at the meso level. As a boundary object, transformative assessment includes and connects the views of the child, the teacher and the parent as well as other potential actors across places and institutions and over time. In this process, different actors also acquire values and views from those around them, and the 'assessment is overtaken' (cf. 'action is overtaken' in Latour, 2005), mixed and transformed (see learning stories in Chapters 3 and 5).

We can also mention specific health care documents as a further example of assessment as a boundary object between ECE, home and another institution. There are forms of collaboration in which the child's development (for example, in motor skills and in language acquisition) is assessed and tested in ECE and then reported to health care professionals. Hence, the documentation and assessment in some cases carried out by the health care sector is moved into ECE. In the following example (Markström, 2006), the teacher is discussing this kind of assessment with the parent:

TEACHER: When we did the test last year, she could not stand on one leg, but now she can.
PARENT: Okay. Stand on one leg?
TEACHER: Yes, we try to do a test, such as in the health care, you know? They (the children) have to answer questions about different things and draw a person, and we compare the test with what she did last year, and I told her that she was really good at jumping on one leg compared with last year and she was really proud, you know?[3]

The transformative nature of assessment becomes evident also in the relations between ECE, school and home. When the child leaves ECE, her or his portfolio is often given to her or him (to the parent) at a handover talk between ECE representatives, school teachers and parents. Thereafter, the school has the opportunity to have a part of the portfolio in order to meet the child in her or his development. In some cases, the IEP is given to child's parents with the aim of getting them to forward it to the school. Thus, the assessments may be continued from preschool to school. The documentation practice in preschool can also be influenced by the school culture and acquire graded knowledge assessment at the individual level. This can be exemplified by comments such as TRAS helps children when they start school, from teachers.

Furthermore, there are questionnaires intended to measure customer (parent) satisfaction. The parent assessment may then be taken over into preschool, as the teacher in the following interview extract suggests:

TEACHER: Yes, we have had it a couple of times, gave questionnaires to the parents. /.../ Yeah, it is clear that as a teacher, an employed teacher paid by taxpayer's money, I then have a responsibility /.../ I feel that you have a responsibility, both to yourself and to the taxpayer and the customer. I can see things very much from the customer's perspective. So the customer is always right. And it is your job to satisfy them.

Accordingly, if the customer is always right and it is the teacher's job to satisfy her or him, then the teacher can consider the parents' possible desires as guidelines of her assessment work. This illustrates a market and customer orientation that is, on the one hand, important for the functioning of ECE nowadays. On the other hand, it can produce a discrepancy, for example, in relation to the pedagogical aims of the institution.

Transformative assessment as a boundary object between offline and online

The concept of transformative assessment captures also the interplay between documentation and assessment in offline and online modes. The interplay can concern media of three degrees (Bruhn Jensen, 2011). The first degree refers to verbal language or speech, but it includes also song, dance, painting and creative arts, as well as different utensils like pens and musical instruments. Media of the second degree consists of, for example, photography, film, printed books, radio and video – media reproduced technically and materialized. Finally, the digitally processed forms of representation and interaction comprise the media of the third degree for which the computer provides a meta-medium; the third degree offers an infrastructure for the distribution of one-to-one, one-to-many, many-to-one and many-to-many communications (ibid).

In our case study of the three preschools, we moved between online and offline representations of assessment when we examined how assessment is presented in the preschools' homepages and what comprises the non-electronic multi-documentation of the preschools. Different discussion sites on the Internet provide an abundance of examples of a similar kind of movement. These sites provide threads of discussion where the assessment of children that has been carried out offline is transformed to an assessment of parenthood or teachers online (see Chapter 8). This is illuminated in the following example that deals with the individual developmental talk in ECE; the positive assessment of the child is communicated online by the parent and transformed into an assessment of the particular parent by other participants:

MOTHER: I had an IDP-talk with Antonio's responsibility educator. /.../ The educators have observed him for a while now, and (they have) done a few different 'tests' to see where he is developmentally. It has been found that Antonio builds up 4–5 word sentences, goes up the stairs with alternating feet (and) has well-developed gross and fine motor skills. /.../ They had made a building-blocks test, and the hope was that he would stack four blocks, but he stacked sixteen blocks ['Hey, four-year-old!', his teacher laughed when she told me this]. Another test was that he would put out cards with different colours on a colour chart. At his age, it can be tricky to even cope with four pieces, but he had placed all twelve.

COMMENTATOR 1: But wow, he is incredible! But you are also a great mother.

COMMENTATOR 2: Oh, you should feel really proud! You really are my mother role model!

(Allt för föräldrar, 2009)[4]

The following two quotations demonstrate how parents also assess the teacher and the teacher's assessment:

PARENT 1: You do not have to have met that teacher to write back a written assessment: unpedagogical and tactless. Lack of empathy and difficulty in putting across criticism in a constructive way.

(Allt för föräldrar, 2009)

PARENT 2: Our son's day-care has something called TRAS. (It is) completely worthless, and it judges the children, too. The worst thing is that every preschool teacher in preschool assesses completely differently, so, therefore, you never get a full picture of the child. My son was forced to (see) a speech therapist, despite my protests. No one took me seriously because TRAS showed otherwise.

(Familjeliv, 2009)[5]

On the one hand, the two quotations illuminate the position of documentation and assessment as actors as well as their ability to constrain and weaken the parental position, as the parent in the second quotation states, 'no one took me seriously because TRAS showed otherwise'. On the other hand, the examples show how documentation on the Internet can have the potential to empower and strengthen parents, for example, either through the appreciation they receive from other commentators or because of the possibility to make assessments about the teachers or ECE they would perhaps not make offline (for example, 'unpedagogical and tactless').

The concept of documentality underlines the constitutive power of documents and their functioning as the 'politics of truth' (Steyerl, 2003). The documentation practices are both embedded in and produce power relations. Yet, the auditing potential (the possibility to audit the unexpected) of the documentation practices also makes it possible to reveal what is unforeseen in these power relations. The transformation from assessing children offline to assessing teachers online is an interesting example of documentality and power relations; it shows both the constitutive power of documents as the 'politics of truth' and the challenging or resistance of this truth in the otherwise unforeseen transformation between offline and online power relations.

The online documentation can also suggest a transformation of the assessment to the macro level. At this level, the interplay between various forms of documentation and assessment can also involve the state government, science, market and civil spheres (see Chapter 9). Finally, it may be noted that the concept of transformative assessment does not relate to a prescriptive concept (a prescribed ideal, cf. Mezirow et al., 1990; Popham, 2008); instead, it is a descriptive and reflexive concept that enables a critical approach for considering the complexity of documentation and assessment.

The preschool teachers as multi- and trans-actors in multidimensional steering

In the multi-documentation and transformative assessment of ECE, teachers can be defined as *multi-actors* or *trans-actors*, reflective, transformative boundary operators (Vallberg-Roth, 2012b). As trans-actors, teachers can move across elusive and perforated borders between potential relationships and positions with different control and discretion (cf. Berg, 2010). A trans-actor is a teaching subject in educating processes, in a changing mode of re-interpreting and re-creating in different directions and at different levels. Teachers are actors between the documentation and assessment practices at micro, meso and macro levels, where different traditions and influences come into consideration. With a didaktik approach in the documentation and assessment practice, there is movement between diverse contents, forms, actors and functions. When the teachers use different documentation tools they are also switching between diverse desirable subjects based on different sources of knowledge. If this is known by the teacher she may be able to make more informed choices and argue for assessments in balance between human responsibility and accountability (see Chapter 9).

Overall, the professional responsibilities may be described in a movement from liability in trust (responsibility) to responsibility by describing their activities (accountability). Professionally, the intensified responsibility for documentation requires an expanded symbolic competence involving skills to write and speak, to express, to communicate and to account for action (Andersen-Østergaard, Hjort & Skytthe-Kaarsberg-Schmidt, 2008). The challenge is to translate and transform the everyday practices to a symbolic account, but this demands time and reflection. However, based on our findings, a lack of time is, indeed, something the teachers experience, as the following quotation suggests:

TEACHER: There are quite a number of different forms of documentation.
INTERVIEWER: Do you want to say something about the combination of these various forms of documents? Do you have particular thoughts about it?
TEACHER: We need more reflection time together. /.../ We have not had the time to reflect on that.

However, despite the shortage of time, the teachers refer to documentation in a positive manner. There are two main explanations for this. First, the teachers underline the importance and the positive effects of documentation and assessment of children:

TEACHER 1: Yes, we document the development here and the progress the child makes. If they are maybe five-years (-old) and do not say many words, it is still a development. It is supposed to be the positive trend we document.
TEACHER 2: We must emphasize that this is nothing negative. Everything that exists in the portfolio should be positive.

As these quotations infer, the early childhood educators talk about documentation more often as a supporting tool than as a tool of control. Hence, they perceive documentation as being in the child's best interest. Additionally, it is almost always the children that are the objects of observation and documentation (cf. Andersen-Østergaard et al., 2008). The majority of the documentation tools are designed for this purpose.[6]

Second, documentation has a positive value because it is associated with professionalism. Andersen-Østergaard et al. (2008) note that documentation and evaluation are predominantly perceived as relatively neutral activities that make learning visible without affecting it. This notion can also create a basis for strengthening the professional status of documentation. This is also evident in our studies: documentation can be seen as a tool for professionalism and as a support in carrying out the teacher's mission. The following two quotations illustrate this notion:

TEACHER 1: I can say that I have absolutely no criticism against documentation. I think it is my profession; it is my pleasure. It is my job to document for myself and for the children. But /.../ when we started, we had 13 children in a children's group; we were 3 in staff, at least back then. Then we had 15, so we got 16, then we had 17, (and) now we have 20 children between 1 to 5 years (of age). So, we do not retain any 6-year-olds, /.../ which we also had in our activities in the past. The burden, responsibility and safety thinking has grown so much in my role as a preschool teacher. Actually, I might not like that that is my role /.../ as a preschool teacher. I have absolutely nothing against documentation; that is what I would like to work with. That is what I think is my job.

TEACHER 2: Not assessment, but I link professionalism in documentation. I believe that the one is necessary for the other to work. I think it is hard to be professional in everything you do if you do not have documentation.

The teachers' answers can be understood as an illumination of Ferraris' (2013) argument that social objects are constructed by inscription (or institutional objects by documentation). According to the replies, professionalism (social object) is not possible without documentation (inscription).

Andersen-Østergaard et al. (2008) argue that the consistently positive and 'neutral' stance regarding documentation can lead to a false or deceptive picture that reinforces an idealized representation of educational work. The authors state that the image constructed by documentation can be quite far from the spontaneous and complex processes of everyday life in educational institutions with their embedded contradictions and conflicts. Overall, our studies suggest that teachers need to develop competence in critically approaching assessment and documentation. A critical approach could be characterized as interplay between believing and doubting games. The doubting game is used in order to scrutinize and test, while the believing game is in contrast a disciplined practice of trying to be as accepting as possible to new ideas (Elbow, 2008, p. 1).

Transformative assessment in multi-documentation – summing up

This chapter has presented the concept of transformative assessment to capture the complexity of multi-documentation in contemporary Nordic ECE with its different contents, forms, actors and functions. The discussion of the concept draws on the notions of summative and formative assessment and documentality. Transformative assessment is a concept focusing on reshaping and interplaying assessments that are intertwined in the registration and complex documentation in preschools. Varying ways to record – whether written or in the form of pictures, videos or symbols – shape and reshape different versions of reality as an expression of power. All assessments in documentation are formed from specific positions, interests and perspectives, and they influence how reality is constructed and performed. Transformative assessment may interact between different theoretical positions and assemblies, including influences from psychological, socio-cultural, market economy (goal–result–quality), neuroscience and post-humanist approaches. Transformative assessment may be seen as an assessment in interplay between different actors, forms, content and functions. The assessment moves and makes connections across boundaries on different levels in complex networks, both offline and online. Transformative assessment can be regarded as interplay between linear (goal-directed) and non-linear (rhizomatic) assessment, and between punctual and processual assessment. The assessment is part of an interwoven and on-going transformation in a multidimensional steering at micro, meso and macro levels. The macro level is related to the state, science, the market and the civil sphere (see Chapter 8 and 9).

Based on the presented complex documentation and assessment practice, teachers can be described as multi-actors or trans-actors, as reflective and transformative boundary operators in multi-documentation. In a didaktik approach, teachers as trans-actors concerns critical thinking, leading to a professional assessment and documentation practice in interplay between believing and doubting games. On the one hand, teachers may be critical and search for signs of power relations; on the other hand, they may search for unexpected, not yet known, possible and potential development and change.

Notes

1 The chapter is partly based on the articles Vallberg-Roth (2011b) and (2012b).
2 Bildung processes are about preparing individuals for an open future. Theories of Bildung emphasize the development of individual thoughts and initiatives. The growing human being needs to develop a personal and independent attitude to his or her own culture. This includes learning to see the specific cultural, political and economic interests behind the prevailing order, but it can also include comprehending that certain disciplines and theoretical traditions do not formulate questions in a totally disinterested manner (Uljens, 1997, 2006).
3 These kinds of tests are based on standardized age-related norms connected to developmental psychology, which may be interpreted as incompatible with the policy in Swedish preschools but may be compatible with the Anglo-Saxon tradition (see Chapters 2 and 3).
4 The material is from the communities 'Allt för föräldrar – Din familj på nätet' ('Everything for parents – Your family on the net') and 'Familjeliv' ('Family life') begun in 2003. The online communities are said to have many members. It is important to remember that on the Internet anyone can pretend to be, for example, a parent. The threads from the online communities are initiated by the participants and often involve communication between two or three, and sometimes up to five or six, people.

5   See note 4.
6   Thus, our answer to the didaktik question about who assesses whom would be: the teacher does it to the child. In a few cases, there are also descriptions of older children documenting one another. It is evident, though, that the documentation does not concentrate on teachers. As one of the teachers said, 'filming adults is a much more sensitive approach'. Our material shows that the gaze of documentation targeted at children and their learning processes is only unwillingly directed toward the teachers. However, the teachers' reflection on the documentation of children can also focus on the educators' approach in the form of a self-assessment. It can invite considerations concerning why the teacher chose to observe a specific situation, how she/he did it, and how she or he plans to use it with the children and in her/his work.

PART II
Auditing the child

The following two chapters examine the documentation and assessment of children by applying the perspective of social studies of childhood. This means they share an interest in questions, such as, how children are constituted – or subjectified in Foucauldian terms – in social and institutional practices, and how they are positioned in intergenerational relations. Consequently, the chapters depart from the pedagogically-oriented discussions of child documentation, though they are not at all extraneous of pedagogy. The first of the chapters, Chapter 5, discusses the impetus of many, especially open, tools of child documentation, that is, listening to the child. This impetus reflects the democratic aims of documentation and the statutory demands of accounting for the child's views according to the UN Convention on the Rights of the Child. Chapter 6 focuses on the constraints that the institutional order of ECE poses on children by examining the notions of the 'normal' child in documentalized practices. Both chapters are principally based on data from parent–teacher discussions. Considering the focus of these discussions – the child as an individual – the findings may at first glance look discouraging. Listening to the child seems to turn into lip service and the focus on the individual seems to change to communication aiming at normalization. However, the aim is not to suggest that ECE is not seriously striving to fulfil its objectives. Rather, the findings illuminate how we are cultural beings and live by the dominant discourses of our culture. All the same, we can also strive to become more aware of our own notions and their effects on our conduct.

5

DOCUMENTATION AND LISTENING TO THE CHILDREN

'To ensure listening and being listened to is one of the primary tasks of documentation' Rinaldi (2005, p. 23) argues when discussing pedagogical documentation in the Reggio Emilia style. The same idea is salient in many other approaches to documentation regardless of their theoretical foundations. It is, for example, found in learning stories, which are a narrative assessment practice that emphasizes dialogue (Carr & Lee, 2012). Listening through documentation is also a common practice when the primary focus is not on learning processes but on supporting children's participation in education more generally. The Mosaic approach, for example, combines observation, interviewing and participatory tools to listen to young children's perspectives (Clark, 2005).

The notion of listening to children is intertwined with the idea of the competent and agentic child, a conception that is common in contemporary (Nordic) early childhood education (ECE) (James, 2012; Kampmann, 2004; Kjørholt, 2005; Lenz-Taguchi, 2010; Vandenbroeck & Bouverne-De Bie, 2006). For example, in Reggio Emilia, the child is not seen as 'fragile, needy and incapable', but as 'competent and strong' and as an 'active subject' (Rinaldi, 2005, p. 19). Learning stories are grounded in the idea of a child who is both a participant with agency and an authoritative and accountable learner (Carr & Lee, 2012). In short, the basis of documentation is often the child as an individual, who is understood as worth listening to because of her or his competence to express her or his wishes, interests and inner moods in rational ways (Kampmann, 2004, pp. 137–48; Kjørholt, 2005; Vandenbroeck & Bouverne-De Bie, 2006). Hence, documentation commonly assumes a child with a 'voice'.

Besides providing means to reach the 'voice' of the competent, agentic and active child, documentation transforms the child's perspective into situations in which adults discuss it among themselves. For example, Rinaldi (2005) describes how pedagogical documentation as visible listening enables the revisiting of learning

ɑ also with parents, other educators and com-
ɑnner, learning stories and documentation that
ɾe generally are often shared among educators and
ugh documentation the child's 'voice' becomes an
ɑtional and professional practices.
 interested in the process of the transformation described
ɑt happens when the child's documented views are trans-
ɑon between adults, specifically focusing on how they are
ɑcussion between parents and educators. To illuminate the process
an empirical example from a study on teacher–parent meetings
child's individual educational plan (IEP) in Finnish ECE (Alasuutari,
ɑill focus on children's voices quite 'literally'; that is, we examine how
documented views and often 'quoted' talk are discussed in parent–
interaction. Based on this examination, we problematize straightforward
ɑns of listening to children through ECE documentation.

Before moving on to our empirical examples, we present two opposing notions
of listening to children that are evident in present-day ECE: the naturalistic
approach and the relational approach. The latter provides the starting point for our
empirical examination, which is introduced after first presenting these two
approaches. Finally, we will conclude the chapter by considering the agency and
constraints of documents in transmitting children's perspectives.

The naturalistic approach

Let us consider the following discussion between a mother and a teacher. The
episode comes from a meeting in which the parties were drawing up an IEP for
the child. It starts with the mother's question about the composition of the staff in the
ECE centre the previous day. She justifies her question by referring to what her
son, Ron, had talked about.

MOTHER: Was there someone else (staff member) here yesterday
TEACHER: [Yesterday there was
MOTHER: [Yesterday, generally, 'cause Ron said to me that now we have a totally
    new auntie [a new auntie (imitating the child's voice) and I said that
TEACHER: [Not totally new (with a laughing voice)
MOTHER: Well [surely not
TEACHER: [Yeah (laughing)
MOTHER: Not because someone would have told me something (laughing)

The episode proceeds with the mother elaborating Ron's talk further. She also again
imitates his words about the new 'auntie'. The teacher explains the reasons why they
had a replacement in the class and where the two staff members were the previous
day. With a laughing voice she also points out that the child's view of the arrangement
being permanent was funny. Finally, she makes a reference to documentation.

TEACHER: I'll write it here that we'll talk more about that (staff changes) with the children.

In the above example, the mother's report and imitation of Ron's talk are taken as a factual description of what he has actually said. Naturally, trusting the mother's talk is the basis for a functional interaction between the teacher and the mother. Besides being a factual report of what Ron has said, the talk is assumed to reflect Ron's thoughts and the meanings he has given to the change of staff. Hence, his talk – as the mother reports it – is understood as mirroring his inner self. This is evident, for example, in the teacher's comment about making a note for future action. Registering the issue suggests that Ron's talk is taken as a valid depiction of children's perspectives which the educators need to allow for.[1]

The above example represents a naturalistic approach to language and, consequently, to the notion of listening to children; that is, an approach that we typically apply in orienting to our everyday life and its social relations. The assumption about language as a 'screen' of our mental life is elementary in it. We consider ourselves and other human beings as 'bounded selves' (Gergen, 2009) with individual emotions, experiences, thoughts, mental abilities, intentions and needs. We also recognize children's autonomous inner self (e.g. Kjørholt, 2005), even though, compared with adults, we often consider children as minor in their abilities. According to the naturalistic approach, language serves as our main means to convey our inner life to other people. Consequently, by carefully recording language and talk, the inner life of a person can be (objectively) documented. In research literature, this approach has been labelled, for example, emotionalism (Silverman, 2006), naturalism (Gubrium & Holstein, 1997) and factualism (Alasuutari, 1998).

The relational approach

Even though we usually find the naturalistic approach to 'voice' functional in our everyday life, it has been challenged in the research literature. This criticism principally concerns the assumptions about the authenticity of a voice and the function of language as a mirror to reality. For example, Allison James (2007) questions the authenticity of children's perspectives in childhood studies and states that 'as writers of texts, it is adults who retain control over which children's voices are given prominence and over which parts of what children have to say are to be presented' (ibid., p. 265). Also Spyros Spyrou (2011) underlines the adults' role and the issues of power in interpreting children's perspectives. According to him, 'all reporting of children's voices /.../ is a situated and hence interested representation' (ibid., p. 160). Hanne Warming (2005) goes even further and questions the ontological existence of children's experiences and views, and defines them as contextual.

Even though the criticism described above concerns mainly research, it is relevant also regarding documentation in ECE. The next example illuminates this. In it, the teacher and the mother discuss questions that parents are instructed to talk about with the child before meeting with the teacher. The mother has followed the instructions given and written the child's answers on a specific form. The questions are labelled as 'the child's feedback', and one of them concerns issues in ECE, about which the child is either anxious or concerned or which make the child laugh. At the beginning of the extract the teacher reads aloud the child's answer to this question.

TEACHER: Here is the child's feedback okay. We sang (reads the answer from the form).
MOTHER: Singing that's something she likes.
TEACHER: Yeah, we do sing every day and they all like it a lot.

The child's answer – singing – states an activity common in ECE. However, this does not imply its value from the child's perspective – whether singing is something that the child likes or dislikes. The mother interprets the answer as a positive appraisal of the activity, and the teacher further confirms this by stating that all children feel the same way. Hence, the child's answer has been given a meaning by the adults in a process of co-construction.[2] This meaning-making process, however, is not contingent or conditioned only by the child's answer. Instead, it is framed by institutional aspects and the institutional positions of the parties, as will be shown later in this chapter.

Criticisms of the natural approach are often grounded in constructionist thinking that takes a very different stance toward the function of language. In constructionism, language is not regarded as a reflection of the individual's inner self or as an objective picture of the state of affairs, but is considered as constitutive of our world and ourselves (e.g. Burr, 2003; Gergen, 1999). According to the constructionist approach, when talking about oneself, a person is not primarily reporting on her or his emotions, experiences and perspectives, but constructing them. As Gergen (2009, p. 31) states, 'the individual self is not a state of nature but of language'. Furthermore, constructionism underlines the importance of the context; no utterance has a pure meaning in itself. Instead, its meaning is situational and connected both to the immediate discursive environment and to the broader interactional, institutional, cultural and material context. Moreover, each utterance, text and narration is also situated in relation to the (assumed) recipient. This is also evident in the following learning story quoted from Carr and Lee (2012). It is one of the numerous stories – that is, written narratives – that the authors present as examples of the assessment practice of learning stories.

Ilaria, Isabella and Katharine's Learning Story

We have been reading stories about Percy the Park Keeper and you decided to make a home for the woodland animals. I really enjoyed watching your tree-house spread and grow. You thought carefully about building a place for all the different animals. /.../ You worked very well together /.../

What learning is happening here?

Ilaria, Isabella and Katharine worked very well together, spending time making improvements to their building. They had an excellent use of descriptive language and were able to introduce a story line into their play.

Opportunities and possibilities

Ilaria, Isabella and Katharine are enjoying reading stories about Percy the Park Keeper and learning about different environments that animals live in. We will continue to look at the types of environments that woodland animals live in /.../

Parent comments

Isabella told me she really enjoyed making this home and was able to explain what she had done to make the construction strong.

(Ibid., p. 52)

The apparent recipients of the first part of the learning story are the three children mentioned in its title. The text is written so that it could be read aloud to the children. As such, it can be understood as supporting the revisiting of the story, which is emphasized in learning stories to make children recognize their 'learning journey' (ibid., p. 9). The second and the third parts of the story are more adult in style. The second part reports and assesses the three children's learning as a joint process and seems to be addressed to the adult audience interested in a specific learning process or in the learning outcomes of the institution generally (parents, other educators, administrators). The third part orientates to the educators of the institution ('we'), but it can also be seen as a report to other parties interested in the educational work of the institution. The last part of the story includes text from one of the girls' parents. It seems to be written as a message to the educators. (If the authors of the story – the teacher and the parent – had known that the story will be used for the particular book, we could assume that the story has also been shaped according to the book's assumed audience.) In all, the learning story shows how there is no authoring without audience (cf. Chapter 3). What is written or documented always assumes some readership (Buchanan and Dawson, 2007; Garfinkel, 1984, pp. 186–207; Vásquez, 2009).

The relational and constructionist approaches are not new in ECE documentation. Gunilla Dahlberg, Peter Moss and Alan Pence (2007, p. 147), for example, underline that pedagogical documentation does not represent a true reality and that it does not exist apart from the educator's involvement (see also Chapter 3). According to them, meaning is co-constructed in pedagogical documentation. In learning stories (Carr & Lee, 2012), the construction of learning dispositions and learner identities are underlined. Following the post-humanist approach (see Chapter 1), Lenz-Taguchi (2010) argues for an 'onto-epistemological' thinking that underlines the 'intra-action' of the material, discursive and human beings in the construction of knowledge. She seems to draw on both the realistic and the constructionist approaches. She underlines the agency of the material world, but also states that 'pedagogical documentation is not about documenting the practice as a representation' (ibid., p. 63). Instead, 'documentations can be understood as having agency of their own' (Lenz-Taguchi, 2010, p. 88); they do and perform issues in relation to the pedagogical practice.

These few references already show that the constructionist ideas are applied in different ways. Constructionism is not one specific approach but takes many forms in educational literature and in scientific discussion more generally (see Holstein & Gubrium, 2007). Sometimes the terms constructivism and constructionism are also used as synonyms, even though they are usually understood as differing from each other. Both terms underline the role of culturally- and historically-conditioned discourses in constructing the world for us. However, constructivism leans more on cognitivism and on the notion of the individual mind, while constructionism emphasizes interaction and locates the meaning-making process in social practices (Sparkes & Smith, 2007). Next we will apply the constructionist approach – thus, the relational view on the child's voice – and highlight how the child's documented views of ECE-related issues are negotiated in parent–teacher discussions.

Dealing with the child's views: a case example

Our case study comes from Finnish ECE (Alasuutari, 2013) and applies naturally-occurring data: that is, specific parts of tape-recorded parent–teacher discussions about the child's individual educational plan (IEP) and the corresponding IEP documents. These discussions are a common practice in Finnish ECE and they are usually structured by a form (see Alasuutari & Karila, 2010). In our examination we will focus on interaction episodes, in which the parent and the teacher discuss questions addressed to the child in the IEP form. Hence, they focus on the child's views. The questions include inquiries such as: 'Tell about yourself in your own words'; 'What do you expect and wish for from being in day care?';[3] 'Is there something that you do not like in day care?'; 'Is there something that makes you anxious, bothers you or annoys you in day care?'; 'What do you like to do in day care?; and 'Whom do you like to play with?'[4] The parent is expected to present the questions to the child and document the answers on the IEP form before meeting with the teacher. Our main interest lies in how the child's documented answers are treated in the interaction; in other words, how they affect the discussion between the parent and the teacher and convey the child's views.[5] For the sake of simplicity, we address the documented responses of the child by referring to them as 'answers', 'views' and 'perspectives', even though we consider them as co-constructions. Following mainly the theory of documentality (Ferraris, 2013), but also the ideas presented in Action Network Theory (Latour, 2005) and those presented by Prior (2003), we examine the forms as agents in interaction with human agents (cf. intra-action in Lenz-Taguchi, 2010).

The easy answers

The findings of the case study show that while some of the answers received to the questions posed to the child seem to be easy for the parties to discuss, some suggest interactional tensions. Moreover, there are two types of easy answers: the first one includes stories or pictures produced by children, and the second comprises responses that describe common ECE activities such as playing, singing or being with friends as enjoyable and amusing for the child. These answers are shown consistent appreciation in the parent–teacher interaction, albeit in different ways.

Below is an example that concerns the first type of answers. It is from a discussion about a four-year-old girl, Ida. In her IEP form there is a long answer to the query in which the child is asked to tell about her- or himself. The answer starts in the following way: 'I am Ida. I can dance ballet. I have a blond hair. I also like football. I like movies.' Then the answer continues with a long story about a worm. In the meeting the beginning of the answer is not discussed at all but the teacher reads aloud the story and the mother makes some comments in between her reading. The interaction episode is long and it ends with the teacher's following turn of talk:

TEACHER: Yeah, okay, oh no (laughs). This (story) is just lovely but it like depicts, I think, Ida just so well. She has imagination. We'll see what she'll be one day.

In this example, as in the other interaction episodes about children's drawings and stories in the data, the child's answer produces laughter and seems to amuse the adults. Usually the story or the drawing is characterized as 'lovely' by the teacher, as in Ida's case. Hence, the adults show appreciation to the child's response in their interaction and seem to value it, although primarily as an artefact. This means that the story or the drawing is evaluated or that the child's skills are assessed on the basis of it. However, the participants do not discuss what implications the answer may have for the child's early education (for example, Ida's interest in football and ballet in her answer). Thus, the interaction following the first type of easy answers positions the child and/or her output as an object of assessment. This again produces a generational demarcation between the child and the adults competent to assess her or him.

In the second type of easy answers – that is, the answers describing ECE activities in a positive tone – the adults again show appreciation to the child's views but position the child differently. The next example illustrates this type of answer. It comes from a discussion between the teacher, the mother and the father who talk about a three-year-old, Mathias. To the question 'What else does the child want to tell about day care?', one of the parents wrote the following answer: 'I like to be in day care. I like to play'. In the meeting, the teacher starts the discussion of the question by topicalizing the last sentence of the answer.

TEACHER: Yes and here one surely sees that playing is awesomely important, it is, like, for the whole group /.../ All of them (children) would just like to play. In the morning circle they always ask if they can already go playing (laughs)

FATHER: Yeah I also always /.../ when I come to pick him up I always ask if he
    had fun and what they had played
MOTHER: Yeah, uhum
FATHER: Those are the most important (things).

In her response the teacher generalizes the child's answer to concern all children –
they all like playing – and elaborates her response with the example from the morning
circle. Thus, she validates and confirms the child's answer as being right and informative or knowledgeable about what it means to be a child in ECE. The teacher's
response produces, and is founded in, her position as a professional who knows ECE
and children. In his turns of talk, the father also shows his knowledge about the importance of play to his son. The mother expresses her support to the father's view.

The discussion about Mathias's response exemplifies typical interaction between
the teacher and the parents in our data when the child's answer describes ECE
activities in a positive tone. The interaction can be characterized as a negotiation
in which both parties present a description that validates the child's view. The
teachers confirm the child's answer by generalizing it to other children, as in
Mathias's case, or by explaining how the specific activity is emphasized in the curriculum or activity plan of the child group, as in the example about singing above.
The parents validate the answer usually by describing the child's similar behaviour
or interests at home. The negotiation produces an alignment and an appreciation
of the child's answer. At the same time, the child's knowledge about her or his life
is acknowledged. Moreover, in the negotiation, the adults jointly construct their
institutional roles: the teacher who is an expert in early education, children's
behaviour and development, and the parent who knows her or his child and is
collaborative.

The two types of easy answers seem to lead to two different end results regarding the child's position and views. In the first type, the child is mainly positioned
as an object of assessment. In the second type of answers, assessment is also present,
but the child's knowledge of her or his own life is acknowledged. Thus, the child
is positioned as competent in assessing her or his situation. In the interaction episodes it is evident, however, that the child's response is not dealt in a 'vacuum'.
Instead, generational ordering (Alanen, 2009) – that is, notions of traditional differences in competences between adults and children – and institutional discourses
framing the position, notions of knowledge and expertise, and participation of the
parties condition the discussion regarding the child's answers.

The difficult answers

The difficult answers by children are very similar in their content. Most of them
deal with bullying and hitting, and a couple of them concern daily naps. Typically
they are very short and none of them describe, for example, hitting as a continuous
problem in ECE. However, what is common to all of them is the implication that,
from the child's perspective, unpleasant issues or occasions do occur in ECE.

The following answer by a three-year-old, Nikolas, is a typical example. It has been written as a response to the questions: 'Is the child anxious about something in day care, is (s)he annoyed by something, is (s)he being bullied, what makes her/ him laugh?'. The answer goes: 'Not annoyed, if someone hits me then I'll start to cry. When I am tickled I'll start to laugh'. In the parent–teacher meeting the response becomes topical when the teacher reads it from the IEP form. After reading the sentence about hitting, the teacher continues:

TEACHER: But seldom in this kind of situation has there been any crying, though. Naturally there's been some minor pushing and [such always then
MOTHER: [Yeah, yeah
TEACHER: but Nikolas seems to defend himself if not otherwise then at least verbally. He doesn't necessarily immediately push back but
MOTHER: Uhum
FATHER: Yeah, no he doesn't. At some point he defended himself too little.

The teacher immediately states that Nikolas's answer about hitting does not quite describe the actual situation: when there has been 'minor pushing', Nikolas has not usually cried but defended himself. Hence, the teacher refutes Nikolas's response and both of the parents show their (apparent) alignment with this, the father by commenting on his son's ways of defending himself and the mother by minimal feedback tokens (yeah, uhum).

As in Nikolas's case, the children's responses about hitting and bullying are refuted or invalidated in the parent–teacher interaction in our data. In the above example we cannot yet quite see why this occurs. However, as the discussion continues, it illuminates the interactional process more thoroughly. After a short discussion about Nikolas's abilities to defend himself, the father raises again the topic of hitting and bullying.

FATHER: Yesterday he said something about it, it seemed that there had been some competition about (snow) horses outside and then they (the children) had kind of pushed each other away (from the horses) alternately. That's how I understood it like
MOTHER: (Laughs) Uhum
TEACHER: Yeah, yeah (with a laughing voice). No, wasn't it a, what was it, a seal there at the other side of the yard
FATHER: Yeah
TEACHER: They did take turns and no one was pushed away from it, at least not in the afternoon (with a laughing voice)
MOTHER: Uhum (with a laughing voice)
TEACHER: You can get quite a nice picture of how it happened (laughing)
FATHER: Yeah, no it is mainly just like
TEACHER: Yeah, right
FATHER: I think that it's just play anyway.

The father raises the topic of hitting carefully. He does not present it as an obvious fact but refers to his own interpretation of Nikolas's talk. No hitting and bullying is one of the explicit rules of Finnish ECE (Alasuutari & Markström, 2011) and, therefore, suggestions about its occurrence can be understood as a morally-laden and sensitive topic in parent–teacher discussions. The father's cautious way of putting his words can be seen as reflecting this and implying the avoidance of criticizing ECE. The subsequent interaction suggests, however, that his description of Nikolas's talk is dealt with as criticism. First the mother lightens the tone of the father's description by laughter and, hence, implies that the child's description can be taken as humorous (Alasuutari, 2009; Haakana, 2001). The teacher continues with a laughing voice and explains the 'reality' of the incident from the previous day by referring implicitly to her own observations ('at least not in the afternoon'). She also hints at how the parents can get a distorted picture of the incident from the child but presents her statement again with a laughing voice and, hence, with humour. Thus, in her turns of talk, the teacher invalidates Nikolas's talk. The mother seems to align with her talk in her feedback and laughter. At the end of the example, the father also interprets the incident as being children's play.

All the children's responses concerning hitting and bullying or issues that can otherwise be interpreted as complaints in our data refer to incidents, not continuous troubles. Regardless of this, they seem to be taken as challenging the idea of ECE as a well-functioning institution and its professionals as mastering their educational role. The challenge posed by the children's answers is shown in the way the parties invalidate it. The teachers play the main role in this. They deploy discourses that can be linked with the ideals about Finnish ECE and its professionals. Based on their professional knowledge of ECE and children, they explain how the child's answer does not depict the reality. Parents support teachers' views either by short comments or by giving accounts that align with the teacher's description. Hence, they position themselves as collaborative partners and, at the same time, support the teacher's and the institution's 'face'; that is, they do 'face work' (Goffman, 1967)[6] and (re-)produce ECE as a quality institution. As a result, the adults produce a seemingly shared picture of the state of affairs that invalidates the child's response.[7] It is not acknowledged as a valid or adequate description of the child's life. Instead, demarcating the 'accurate' adult view and the 'inaccurate' perspective of the child produces a generational ordering.

Conclusion

The agentic, participative and competent child is a common notion in various practices of documentation in the present-day ECE. The notion is linked with the aims of 'giving children a voice' and accounting for their views through documentation. At the beginning of the chapter we presented two approaches to this: the naturalistic approach that treats the child's expressions as a reflection of her or his inner self, and the relational approach that considers them as interactional co-constructions in a specific context. Even though people usually apply the naturalistic approach as their orientation to everyday life with success, we argued for a relational approach to considering documentation. To illuminate the relational processes that can intertwine in child documentation, we presented a case example from Finnish ECE.

Our example did not focus on documenting children as part of the pedagogical work of ECE, which is usually the context of discussions about the relational nature of child documentation (e.g. Dahlberg et al., 2007). Instead, the case example focused on a very common phenomenon in ECE: the transmission of children's views through documentation into interaction between parents and educators. Specifically, it examined how children's responses to specific 'child questions' were negotiated in a meeting where the parties discussed the child's IEP. Even though the case example itself is limited contextually, it cannot be considered as unique, since the phenomenon it examined is common. For example, our Swedish data shows that very similar kinds of child interviews and questions are discussed on a regular basis in parent–teacher meetings in local preschools. Overall, it is typical that different documentation methods, such as pedagogical documentation (e.g. Rinaldi, 2005), learning stories (Carr & Lee, 2012) and portfolios, are used not just among educators but also as material for meetings with parents (see Chapter 7).

In its detailed findings, however, the case example is restricted. Based on it, we cannot draw conclusions about how bullying is dealt with in Finnish ECE, for example. Nevertheless, conceptually, our examination illuminates issues that can be considered relevant in a more general sense. Especially, questions concerning the agency of documents and their function in the transmission of children's views are important to point out.

The questions addressed to the child in the IEP form in our case example assume a child that knows her or his life and is an agent in it. In the light of documentality (Ferraris, 2013), the form can therefore be seen as an agent in constructing a 'knowledgeable' child. However, our results show that only when the child's response was in line with the institutional discourses – that is, when it expressed a positive picture of the institution – this notion was also produced in the interaction. Hence, even though the IEP form suggested a specific discourse of the child, the agency of the documentation was dependent on how the human beings – especially the teachers in their institutional position as the 'chairs' of the meeting – appropriated them (cf. Cooren, 2004).

In the negotiations about the children's responses, the teachers deployed as their main resource institutional discourses reproducing the ideals of Finnish ECE as a high quality and professional institution. The parents seemed to align with these discourses and with the ideas about collaboration, partnership, and involved and knowledgeable parenthood that are valued in Finnish ECE and culture (e.g. Alasuutari, 2003, 2010b; Stakes, 2004, p. 28) The notions of generational order, produced on the possibilities and rights of the adults and the child to know about the child's living, also played an important part in the negotiations of the child's response. When a response challenged the notion of ECE as a quality institution, the entwined use of the different discourses and notions invalidated the child's answer and, thus, refuted the notion of the knowledgeable child provided by the IEP document. In these situations the interactional aspects conditioning the negotiation also became salient. The different discourses served as resources in face work (see Goffman, 1967), that is, in keeping up and reproducing the institutional discourses of quality ECE. Thus, the use of institutional discourses and the discourses regarding generational relations and parenthood entangled with the demands of face-to-face interaction in an institutional encounter constrained the agency of documentation.

The analysis of the inclusion of the child's views in the parent–teacher discussion exemplifies how the meaning of child documentation is negotiated and 'translated' whenever the documentation is revisited. In interaction, the use of documentation can be seen as a turn of talk that orientates what comes after it. However, it does not necessitate or determine what follows, but its meaning is constructed only in the subsequent talk (e.g. Hepburn and Potter, 2004). The construction – that is, the translation and, consequently, the agency of the documentation – is conditioned and constrained by dominant discourses and situational factors.

These findings can also be related to the concepts of 'weak' and 'strong' documents described by Ferraris (2013, pp. 267–71). Weak documents include a mere registration of issues, but strong documents are performatives that change the state of affairs. However, no document is weak or strong as such; its nature depends on its use (see Chapter 1). In our case example, the child questions in the IEP form followed the underlying value of Finnish ECE in their aim to 'give due weight to the views of the child' (Stakes, 2004, p. 13). However, they did not seem to make much difference in the interactions under scrutiny; thus, in our study it is difficult to call the child questions of the IEP form a strong document. There were only few occasions in which it was implied that the documentation of the child's view might lead to educational acts. Mostly the children's answers were treated as registrations of either a factual issue like enjoying ECE activities or of an incorrect child perspective.

In all, this chapter illuminates the multitude of challenges in documenting children's perspectives. These challenges are not limited to learning how to do the actual documentation and how to be reflective on one's frames of making sense of children's talk and behaviour. They also include broad issues related to interaction in different institutional contexts. Our case example only considered the transmission of the child's views to parent–teacher discussions; however, the interactional aspects are as relevant in encounters among educators, even though the specific discourses and notions that are applied as recourses in them naturally vary.

Notes

1   The use of laughter in the interaction episode described suggests that the mother's talk is taken and dealt with as criticism of the practices of the ECE setting (see Alasuutari, 2009). This can also be linked with the teacher making a note about the future actions regarding talking with children about the changes in staff.

2   Following the relational approach, the child's documented response in the example cannot be considered as objective information about her thoughts and ideas. Instead, the

answer needs to be regarded as a text that has been produced by the parent and that is fundamentally interactional. How well the text reflects the meanings that the child's responses were given to in the actual parent–child interaction cannot be known.

3   Day care is the term commonly used in vernacular when referring to ECE in Finland.

4   The Swedish preschools from which we have collected data use very similar questions to interview children before parent–teacher meetings (see Chapter 6). In this chapter, however, we focus on the Finnish data because of the availability of the actual IEP documents. Our Swedish data is composed mostly of recordings of the parent–teacher discussions.

5   In the original study (Alasuutari, 2013) the focus was not only on how the child's answers were discussed in the parent–teacher interaction but also on how the questions addressed to the child were negotiated in general. Thus, the study also reports findings concerning questions that were not answered at all. These findings are not, however, examined in this chapter.

6   According to Goffman (1967), 'face' refers to an image of self that is presented in terms of approved social attributes. Face work again is about the maintenance of face in an encounter. It is a condition of the interaction, not its objective.

7   It is important to remember that the argument about the apparent alignment and agreement between the teacher and the parent concerns only the flow of the interaction. Considering the constructionist approach and the discourse analytic methodology, the aim is not say anything about the thinking of the parties or imply, for example, that the parents would present the same views in another interactional context.

6

THE 'NORMAL' CHILD

The previous chapters have presented the multitude of documentation tools and practices used in Nordic early childhood education (ECE). These range from standardized and test-type tools to more open means of documentation, such as interviews with children. The chapters have also illuminated the intertwinement of documentation and assessment. Intertwinement is fairly self-evident in tools that explicitly aim at assessment, but is not so easily recognized when considering, for example, recordings of the child's activities in a portfolio, or constructing a general 'picture' of her or him by means of interviews and observations for a developmental talk or meeting between the teacher and parent(s). While these more open documentation practices are generally regarded as having a positive impact on children's development, learning, well-being and participation in ECE, they are not often scrutinized from the perspective of assessment. However, child rearing, childcare and education always involve elements of examination and correction (Dahlberg, Moss & Pence, 2007; Hundeide, 2006; Rose, 1996b). Like the more specific 'assessment' tools, open or general documentation practices are based on and reflect particular assumptions about the child and what is expected of him or her. That is, they encapsulate the notions of the 'normal' or ordinary ECE child and, like all assessment, have a normative effect. These practices are in focus in this chapter.

Using examples from empirical studies, this chapter illustrates how a child's normality and deviation are produced in different ECE documentation practices and in documentalized parent–teacher collaborations. Hence, it considers documentation as a normalizing practice. The chapter also shows how the notions of the ordinary child (girls or boys) are essentially related to the social and institutional orders of ECE, for example, the norms, rules and interactional practices that constitute and show what the preferred and ordinary child/pupil is like. Like the previous chapter, this chapter is based on a constructionist approach. Hence, we approach normality as a social construction and underline the intertwinement of human and material agents – that is, documentation – for producing an understanding of various phenomena, such as normality, and in affecting the behaviour patterns of the institutional actors. Our empirical examples are based on studies of talks between teachers and parents and the documentation used in them.

In this chapter we first present some theoretical points of departure for how normality can be considered as constructed, as well as previous research concerning assessment and documentation in relation to children and normality. We then discuss the results of our studies on how the 'normal preschool child'[1] is constructed in assessment and documentation practices in ECE settings, and how different communicative tools are used in practice. Finally, we consider how particular assumptions and normalities situated in the ECE settings operate through assessment and documentation.

Institutions and normality

As an institution, ECE is both a socially-constructed and routine-reproduced rule system that establishes identities and activity scripts for such identities (Jepperson, 1991, p. 146). It produces its actors – educators, children and parents – by constraining and empowering them in specific ways. The rule system – or social order – of an institution reflects an underlying rationale, for example about what constitutes desirable qualities and behaviour in the institution (cf. Goffman, 1961). Thus, like any other institution, ECE is based on and produces notions of what is expected from and considered normal for its actors. It 'normalizes' them towards the desirable qualities and aims at controlling actions and identities that deviate from the norm.

In the daily life of an institution, normalization mainly occurs in the routines, practices and use of materialities that are based on the dominant discourses of the institution, but which are not often reflected on. They produce the 'hidden agenda of everyday life' (Markström, 2005, p. 29) by structuring the actions and interactions of the institutional actors according to the institutional rationale, usually without any need for a discussion about or negotiation of this rationale. Therefore, the routines and practices provide a fruitful perspective from which to study how 'normality' is produced and handled in institutions. In addition, it is important to stress that, as these kinds of processes occur in most institutional settings, they are important for professionals to reflect on.

The production of normality necessitates classifications and categorizations. These are also implicit or explicit elements of documentation in an ECE and school context, and central in educational settings in general (Rose, 1996b). Classification and categorization transform children into particular objects of the institution, for instance into a child needing special education, or one requiring extra surveillance (cf. Turmel, 2008). Thus, categorization and classification are also ways of exercising power.

Hundeide (2006) and Rose (1996b) argue that different assessment and documentation practices are part of the social striving to construct an ideal child or a desirable pupil. Previous research shows that discourses which draw on developmental psychology and gender are often deployed as resources in the categorizations and control of children, such as notions of the risk of being a late developer, or having too many characteristics of the opposite sex (Canella, 1997; Dahlberg & Lenz-Taguchi, 1995; Dahlberg et al., 2007; Hultqvist, 1990; James, Jenks & Prout, 1998; Markström, 2005, 2008; Popkewitz, 2003). Accordingly, children's normal development is regarded as something that needs to be monitored and controlled (by assessment and documentation) so that nothing goes wrong. In addition, diagnosing children and pupils, and explaining 'problematic behaviour' as something that derives from the individual rather than from something connected to the environment by drawing on medical or psychological discourses, has become an institutional practice (Hundeide, 2006). Hence, knowledge production and institutional practices like documentation are intimately related (cf. Foucault, 2008). However, assumptions about and categorizations of children are also impregnated by other societal discourses and linked, for example, to families and welfare institutions in general. The expert's 'normalizing gaze' is therefore both informed and governed by dominating discourses and frameworks that either emphasize common and 'natural' criteria for assessing the quality of children's development, or the appropriateness of certain behaviour and skills in a particular setting.

In an institution like ECE, different practices are framed by different discourses. These consequently produce specific normalities in children, for instance in observation and documentation practices, in teacher conferences and in informal and formal meetings between parents and teachers. Hence, ECE allows children to take or resist different positions, for instance as boys or girls (Davies, 1993; Davies & Banks, 1995; Davies & Harré, 1990; Duits, 2008; Rhedding-Jones, 1996; Rodriguez, Pena, Fernandez & Vinuela, 2006; Walkerdine, 1990). The frame or the approach that dominates each social practice is also consequential in terms of the organization of future actions and practices. If one deploys an approach based on an individual's defects, it implies that normalization should focus on education, and treating, correcting or compensating for the undesirable or deviant behaviour. However, in approaches in which individuals' shortcomings are regarded as deriving from the environment, the normalizing gaze is turned towards changes in the environment. What we perceive as knowledge and 'truth' contributes to our use of techniques that control, categorize and regulate, i.e., to our normalization practices such as documentation and assessment. This means that notions about a 'normal' or ordinary child or pupil of an educational institution also condition the notions of the educational institution, its meaning and the pedagogical work undertaken in it (Dahlberg et al., 2007).

The normal 'preschool child'

Early childhood education and school provide settings that embed various practices, processes and interactions in which notions of the child and other categorizations are negotiated. As already indicated, our focus is on parent–teacher meetings and the documentation deployed in them. The meetings are interesting from a research point of view, because, due to their informative role in relation to the parents, they often present a collated picture of the child in the institution. Our studies also show that documentation is an essential part of these meetings.

Previous research shows that in parent–teacher meetings the participants primarily focus on assessing and evaluating the individual child (Alasuutari & Karila, 2010; Baker & Keogh, 1995; Markström, 2009, 2011a; Pillet-Shore, 2003; Silverman, Baker & Keogh, 1998) rather than the institution or the teachers' work. In the following we present some examples from our research in Sweden and Finland into different assessment and documentation practices that illuminate how the documents 'invite' an assessment of the child in parent–teacher meetings, and how their use functions as a normalizing practice in these contexts.

Invitations to assessment

Different documentation tools, such as individual educational and developmental plans (IEPs and IDPs), pedagogical documentation, forms and questionnaires, are commonly used in parent–teacher discussions. They help to structure the discussion and serve as formative tools that inform and govern which qualities, skills, possibilities or challenges a child is supposed to have in the setting. According to our findings, forms are often constructed locally but are nevertheless very similar (Alasuutari & Karila, 2010; Markström, 2009; Markström & Simonsson, 2013). For example, in Sweden there seems to be a shared understanding about how the forms should be designed and formulated. They often include questions that both the parents and teachers are expected to answer, such as the child's preferences at home and in preschool, and the child's opinions on different matters, such as whether the child prefers to play alone or together with peers, and which books the child prefers to 'read' at home. Questions about routines regarding arriving at and departing from preschool are also common (Markström, 2006). These types of questions are very much related to a picture of a child as 'being', and seem to be quite neutral (James & Prout, 1997). However, they implicitly communicate expectations about the child's ability or willingness to play alone or with peers, or parents reading to the child at home; something that can also be interpreted as an assessment of the parent (see Chapter 7).

In some of the ECE settings covered in our studies, the teachers fill in questionnaires or forms together with the child. Some institutions also expect parents to do the same thing at home. Getting information from the child about her or his opinions and experiences typically motivates the documentation. Below is one example of this type of 'questionnaire':

> What do you think about playing outside?
>
> What do you think about your peers in preschool?
>
> What can you influence or decide in preschool?
>
> What are you good at?
>
> What do you think is the best about preschool?

The form and the child's answers are then used as points of departure in the talk between the adults (cf. Chapter 5) about what is regarded as important. This is also a way of comparing the answers the child has given to the teacher and to the parent. The same forms and questions can also be re-used in subsequent meetings with the parent(s), i.e., as part of a process over time (Markström, 2009). The questions probe what is seen as valuable and important in ECE, such as play and peers. By producing talk about these issues, they also facilitate an assessment of the child. In addition, the questions invite self-reflection and self-assessment on the part of the child ('What are you good at?').

Documentation tools often contain more specific and detailed questions, which are both influenced by and draw on discourses of developmental psychology. These are usually structured in themes concerning the child's social, emotional and motoric development. The following example comes from a form that is filled in by parents and teachers jointly during the meeting.

> *Here am I – My strengths – Self-development:*
>
> Play
>
> Social
>
> Emotional
>
> Language
>
> Motoric skills
>
> Creative skills
>
> Cognitive development

The frame of developmental psychology encompasses ideas about the normal course of development and learning, and its criteria. Therefore, documentation such as that in the example is associated with assessment, even though it is only used as a 'descriptive' tool. In the example, assessment is explicitly invited in the questions related to 'my strengths' and 'self-development'. Considering that the parent and the teacher are expected to fill in the form together, the term 'my' can be distracting. On the one hand, the form seems to expect the child to assess him- or herself. On the other hand, the word 'my' can be understood as a rhetorical tool that is child-focused and personal.

Below is yet another example from our data of the documentation that parents and teachers construct together when making their assessments using the same form. It also exemplifies how the assessment often includes the child's character and personality. In the instructions, both the teacher and the parents are asked to 'choose a few qualities that best describe the child's personality and behaviour'. The documentation is further motivated by stating 'The aim of this description is to enrich and deepen the picture of the child for all parties, and hence help to understand the individuality of the child.'

Furthermore, some forms require parents to write down the child's strengths and weaknesses and how they expect the teachers to help the child develop. This implicitly takes the assessment of the deficiencies of the individual child as the point of departure, as well as themes concerning the influence of parents in pre-school. Sometimes parents are invited to assess their child in ways that are more 'playful' in nature. 'Strengths Cards' are an example of this. These are used for activating and supporting parents in their talk about and assessment of their child in conversations with the teacher (see Markström, 2011a). The cards have adjectives written on them, such as 'active', 'independent', 'determined' or 'energetic', but are not connected to any specific context, such as the home, preschool or a specific situation. In practice, parents are asked to choose the cards (from about twenty cards) that best describe their child. This means that it is the parents' task to decide how to interpret and use the pre-defined terms and characteristics, and to categorize and label the child. The following example of the use of such cards is from a meeting between a teacher and a child's parents:

MOTHER: Mm, it is difficult. There are too many cards to choose from.
TEACHER: Yes, but have you decided?
FATHER: Yes.
MOTHER: Mm.
TEACHER: You were very quick I think. Three cards?
FATHER: If we think for too long the wrong words might be chosen.
TEACHER: Exactly. The first card you chose was 'determined', you were very quick. Yes that's right, he is like that. What did you think about when choosing that?
MOTHER: He is determined.
FATHER: When he knows what he wants, he let's us know that (laughter). If he doesn't get what he wants he gets angry.
TEACHER: Yes that's right. Determined and stubborn I would say.
FATHER: One can say that. Maybe. He is like his older sister. They can get very angry with each other.
TEACHER: Yes, I think he is determined and stubborn. When he has decided something, he will not change his mind.
MOTHER: Yes, just like that.

In the example, cards containing an adjective – a seemingly neutral artefact – define the situation, set the agenda and involve the parents in the production of an image of the child. The parent is invited to reflect on her or his experiences of the child. However, the talk (and the construction) of these experiences is constrained by the pre-defined terms and the few adjectives provided. Although the tool invites assessment, it also governs it (and the parent in her or his talk) in a number of different ways. The parents' task is to reflect on their children and to deliver a restricted number of pre-defined characteristics (written text, words on cards) that best fit the child in focus, i.e., define what the child 'is' like and deliver these characteristics to the teacher.

Overall, the different documentation tools that are used in parent–teacher meetings can be interpreted as support for or suggestions as to what the talk could be about. However, like other types of institutional documentation, they manifest and order the activity in certain directions. In interviews with the teachers, they argue that the documents and documentation support the talks and what is talked about (Markström & Simonsson, 2013). The talk and the text are therefore intertwined. The uses and formulations of the documentation tools thus govern the 'gaze', what is seen as important to talk about and how this might be done (Markström, 2011b; Markström & Simonsson, 2013). When used, documentation can transform the values and norms of the institutions; a process that we examine in the next section with regard to notions of the 'normal' child.

Talk about children's resistance to 'normality'

Normality can be talked about explicitly in terms of what is preferred. It can also be discussed in terms of what is not desirable. In addition, expectations can be expressed in negative accounts, for example by stating that someone has not done 'something' that was expected (Tannen, 1993). In line with this, Markström (2010) examined episodes in which preschool teachers talked about a child's resistance (to dominant discourses, cf. Foucault, 1994) to the practitioners and/or institution in the developmental talk. The focus was on the teachers' ways of expressing deviant or undesirable behaviour in the preschool setting. The study examined the ways in which teachers talked about problems, assessments and descriptions of how the child was doing something 'wrong' and showed resistance to the preschool institution and the practitioners in different situations or in general. Five main categories were constructed in the analysis of how teachers talked about children challenging and resisting the practitioners and the institution: physical resistance; social resistance; verbal resistance; emotional resistance; and resistance by rejection. The five categories included implicit critique of the individuals and how they acted in relation to ideals and discourses about a normal child in the specific institutional context.

First, the category of physical resistance includes talk about children's independence and skills regarding their body. As a way of showing physical resistance, the teachers talk about how a child does not want to manage on his or her own and wants 'too much' help. Furthermore, when children do not act as they are expected to (normally) in relation to their age or abilities, they are then talked about as problems. It might be a girl who does not want to dress herself, eat independently or abide by an important rule. Being (physically) in the right place at the right time, for example, sitting in the right place at the dinner table when lunch is served, going to a specific room at a specific time for assembly, or other activities that the child is supposed to take part in, means following the order or 'pedagogy of time and space' (cf. Markström, 2005).

Second, teachers also pay attention to social resistance. They especially focus on play and participation in different social and collective activities. Each child is expected to engage in and maintain good social relations with peers and teachers in the institution. Demonstrating social competence by taking part in different collective activities and following collective rules seems to be very important in the (ECE) institution. This means that the child has to deal with and manage his or her peers and members of staff. Some of the boys and girls in the study are talked about as problematical because they do not conform to this order and prefer to play alone. In addition, there seem to be differences in the ways that boys' and girls' social skills are talked about. When girls are talked about as resistant to the social order in preschool, teachers use concepts like too energetic in their social relations, too dominant, or not having enough distance to other people. In addition, boys who are regarded as provocative are talked about as doing the wrong things at the wrong time in the wrong place, being dominant, determined or not emphatic or social enough in relation to their peers. In view of this, the preschool child has to balance between being socially active and being too active, and improving the group spirit without being too dominant in the ECE setting.

Third, accounts of children's verbal resistance are closely related to those of social resistance, but are given specific emphasis by teachers. Both boys and girls are talked about as verbally resistant. Boys are referred to as being 'too capable' of arguing and negotiating, as well as being noisy and using 'dirty words'. When talking about girls, teachers implicitly present it as problematic if girls protest verbally against something. On such occasions the teachers use terms like cocky and bothersome. The teachers also give examples of girls who are seen as collectively going against the teacher when they do not respond to the teacher's talk or questions. Girls are regarded as acting together and refusing to verbalize what they want to. In the teacher's talk this behaviour is regarded as teasing and provoking the institutional order and the professionals involved in it. Goffman refers to this behaviour as 'collective teasing' against the institutional order (Goffman, 1961).

The teachers also talk about children's emotional resistance. Examples of this include being over sensitive, irritated, shy, unsure of oneself, too self-confident, dependent, too independent and children who cry. It is notable that in the empirical material only a few boys are explicitly described as showing emotional resistance to the teachers. Preschool girls are described as shy, sullen, easily upset or having separation problems. In addition, in contrast to the boys, girls are talked about as being too self-confident or having too strong a will. Over self-confidence is thus regarded as not behaving properly. There seems to be an expectation that preschool children will not be too emotionally independent or too dependent on peers or teachers.

Furthermore, having a positive attitude to preschool seems to be very important. Children who show that they are happy and like to go to preschool are seen as 'good' preschool children. Likewise, when children exhibit separation problems, by crying or showing that they do not want to go to preschool or take part in the activities, it is talked about as a big problem and explained in terms of immaturity.

Finally, it is interpreted as a problem if children reject and ignore the teachers and the institution, even if they do not always openly challenge the staff. If the child does not want to go to preschool, or does not want to be an object of care and withdraws, this can be discussed in a negative tone. The child can also be labelled as reserved, as rejecting the teachers and sometimes also other children. More girls than boys are described in this way in the data. In the following example, the teacher tells a mother that her two-year-old daughter sometimes refuses to talk to the teachers, even in situations where communication is deemed necessary.

TEACHER: Sometimes she doesn't want to talk to us.
MOTHER: Oh yes?
TEACHER: When she has decided not to talk to us she fetches a chair and climbs up on it to reach what she wants on the shelf.
MOTHER: Okay.
TEACHER: She takes the puzzle and you can see her smiling as if to say 'I am so smart. I didn't have to talk or look at her' (the teacher).

In this example, the girl is talked about as showing the teachers that she can manage on her own, which the teachers interpret as a rejection of them. She ignores their care for her, i.e., they are not acknowledged. In a situation like this a small child is expected to ask for help. When this particular child demonstrates independence, it is understood as having little or no trust in the teachers, or as teasing the adults. In addition, in Goffman's (1961, p. 12) terms, it can be said that the child does not break the rules but makes a kind of secondary adjustment. The girl appears to have taken matters into her own hands, 'tries to act out the role of the perfect inmate' (ibid., p. 63) and 'build as much of a free community' for herself as possible (ibid., p. 63). In this case she ignores the teacher's care, which is one of the fundamental ideas of preschool.

As indicated above, some of the utterances show that the teachers have an image of a child who acts in ways that do not directly challenge the staff, but at the same time show indirect resistance to the teachers. That is, the child does not explicitly break the rules and demonstrate what is often reflected in language, namely that he or she is balancing on the edge of what is acceptable for a 'good preschool child'. The child is seen as being well aware of the social order of the institution, and as testing the boundaries by using bodily, social, emotional and verbal abilities and other ways of showing resistance and demonstrating power, individually or jointly with peers. In other words, they make space for themselves and in this way affect and create their daily lives (James et al., 1998; Corsaro, 1997; Markström & Halldén, 2009).

In the analysis, the five categories overlapped to some degree. Some of the portrayals of resistant behaviour could, for instance, be interpreted as both social and emotional abilities. The fact that these categories overlap somewhat, such as social and verbal resistance, and verbal resistance and rejection, also reveals the complexities of human behaviour and the use of concepts (Alasuutari & Markström, 2011; Markström, 2010). The examples illustrate good or bad ways of acting. Some of the children's behaviour is translated in moralistic terms, and the examples of resistance can be interpreted as a list of children's shortcomings. In addition, girls and boys are sometimes talked about in different and traditional terms. This implies that the pictures of proper boys and proper girls differ (Markström & Simonsson, 2011).

The ordinary preschool child

What is talked about and regarded as a preferable way of being a child in the ECE setting? In our studies we found that different (essential) aspects are used to value and determine whether the child is living up to what is expected of a 'normal' preschool child. According to our findings, the 'ordinary child' is supposed to:

- Show adjustment to the generational order, for instance follow the teacher's instructions, orders and guidance.
- Have a trusting and close relationship with the adults, for instance by separating from the parent without crying, accepting the teacher's care and closeness, telling the teacher about her/his experiences, feelings and so on without trying to claim too much of the teacher's attention.
- Have a positive attitude towards the preschool institution and its adults, be happy and interested in the activities provided by the adults, and participate in the activities.
- Show independence and self control by managing her/his body, be aware of her/his skills and needs and communicate these to the teacher.
- Prefer peers and gendered play, i.e., want to be and play with other children and enjoy their company, play with children of the same sex and engage in play that is typical for her/his sex, show concentration in play, defend her- or himself but does not purposely harm or tease other children and solve disagreements in a rational way.

Here the ordinary child is the preschool child; a child that preferably fits into the collective in preschool. Consequently, adapting to the collective order is important in this setting. Moreover, in our Nordic studies we found children's social competence and independence of specific adults and peers in preschool to be the most important skill according to parents and teachers (Alasuutari & Markström, 2011; Granbom, 2011). That is, self regulation and independence seem to be important for a competent child.

According to what has been outlined above, it would seem that teachers have certain images of what preschool children should be like and how they should behave, although there is also space for diversity within certain limitations. The basic elements of the institutional order are very much about becoming a member of a social system and following its core rules and traditions. In addition, the assumptions about favouring the company of peers and being an active participant in the preschool class reveal an expectation of a socially skilled child who is a competent participant in the collective. Hence, becoming social seems to be the key issue in Finnish and Swedish preschools (ECE). Achieving, for example, educational goals or literacy skills are not often talked about. One might ask whether this is a uniquely Nordic phenomenon. Internationally, the preschool's role in supporting a child's readiness for formal learning, reading and writing is often emphasized (cf. Sammons et al., 2004; Taggart, 2004). Recently, more academic goals have become topical in discussions about the Swedish preschool curriculum.

The assumptions that frame the characterizations, evaluations and categorizations are primarily contextual and relate to the preschool's rules, norms, principles, practices and routines. Accordingly, the 'ordinary' child is constructed as one whose conduct meets the institution's expectations and who adjusts to the constraints and possibilities of the institutional role of a preschool child. The adjusting child can either be talked about as a model for other children, or as a child who 'does not need the teachers'.

Observations and documentation of individuals are always informed by values and norms concerning what are seen as normal or desirable in a certain context. Which positions are open to a child in preschool, and what kind of possibilities are there for children to resist the social order and stretch the boundaries? As indicated above, the evaluative accounts show what is preferred in the specific preschool context. Despite this, there are no clear-cut distinctions between the positive or negative pictures of children that are presented, and how normality is negotiated in the talks. That is, when we categorize and classify children in talk and text/documentation, there is a risk that complexity and diversity will be neglected. Predefined forms and problem categories govern the view of and assumptions about individual children, although these can also be blurred and draw on different discourses in situ. Furthermore, as in other social communities, aspects such as age, ethnicity, class and gender are important to take into account in a preschool setting (Lappalainen, 2004).

Conclusions

As discussed in this chapter, the different practices, documentation and meetings and talks between teachers and parents in ECE settings are rich in normative descriptions about the child. They consequently tend to be evaluative and either point to the child in positive terms as active, capable and competent, or as not meeting the expectations of the institution (Alasuutari & Alasuutari, 2012; Alasuutari & Markström, 2011; Markström, 2010, 2011b). In other words, the participants express their expectations, desires and ambitions of individual children in talk and text, and make statements that confirm the child as a 'normal preschool child' or one who should change his or her behaviour in a desirable direction (Alasuutari & Markström, 2011; Markström, 2006, 2009; Pillet-Shore, 2003). In addition, the talks and texts can also be a way of showing and ensuring that the child is seen and receives the support it needs. Although the assessments are both explicit and implicit, they are predominantly implicit. This is something that appears in most institutional talks in different settings and as such cannot be avoided. However, as professionals it is important to reflect on these processes and on the specific ways in which documents are used and transformed.

Studies of developmental talks in ECE have shown how teachers shape their point of departure during the meetings with parents, where talk and text (written forms) are intertwined (Markström, 2009, 2011b). The written text that is used and referred to in these talks is often used to emphasize a particular point. Moreover, when a categorization of an individual is made, it often has a looping effect, i.e., the way we describe someone not only has an impact on how we perceive that person, but also on the 'gaze' and how other individuals are categorized in that setting (Säljö & Hjörne, 2009, p. 96).

The examination of children's behaviour or bodily skills is used as a basis for certain statements and can be built on shifting and temporary ground (Andréasson & Asplund Carlsson, 2009), especially where moral elements are included. For instance, talk about children's resistance both shows and constructs what kind of behaviour and what kind of child is preferred in this context (cf. James et al., 1998; Mazeland & Berenst, 2008). Implicit and explicit utterances about children appear to be embedded in a somewhat rational and instrumental focus or ideal – an 'institutionally situated normality' (Markström, 2005) – and consequently result in a contextual evaluation. Here the focus is on what children need to learn to succeed in this context. It also says something about the ideas and the socialization and regulation processes of an ECE setting. The assumptions that frame the characterizations, evaluations and categorizations could be seen as important elements of the ECE's social order and normalities regarding young children.

The social order of ECE is constructed and based on particular assumptions about the institution's actors, and operates as a constraining, controlling and empowering structure for all its actors in talk and text. Every specific context, such as an ECE institution and its practices, also presumes specific conduct, characteristics and relations of its actors – children, teachers and parents. Consequently, it produces and enables a particular kind of child, and assumes a particular kind of ordinariness and normality in children. In line with this, research on development talks and teachers' utterances concerning children in developmental talks can provide valuable knowledge about the preschool and how practitioners want children in preschool to act and behave, i.e., how to behave in a normal way. However, it is important to stress that there are no 'pure normalities'. These are things that are constructed between the actors, in this case talk, texts and documents.

The findings of the present studies emanate from discussions with adults. Hence, they do not allow any conclusions to be drawn about the behaviour of teachers in their everyday work with children in preschool. However, from the social constructionist viewpoint, they indicate the existence and strength of the discourses as recourse for 'doing' in the teachers' everyday interactions with the children (cf. MacNaughton, 2000; Robinson & Díaz, 2006).

Note

1   In this chapter we use the terms preschool and preschool child when talking about the ECE centres and the children in it, because the empirical data from the Swedish and Finnish ECE context makes use of both these terms.

PART III

Focus on parenthood

In this part of the book we address questions regarding the parent and parenthood in relation to assessment and documentation in ECE. How are parents positioned and how do parents position themselves, online and offline? We invite the reader to consider parents and parenthood vis-á-vis assessment and documentation in two very different contexts: in institutional encounters between the parent and the teacher, and on Internet sites where parents discuss their child's documentation among themselves. The first chapter, Chapter 7, highlights the expectations and demands on parents in the documentalized childhood. We discuss how parents are involved in the different stages of processes of assessment and documentation used to establish collaboration between the home and ECE institution. The chapter exemplifies how different communicative tools are used not only to support, but also to govern the parents' gaze on their own children by drawing on implicit norms of good parenting and good children in the ECE context. The next chapter, Chapter 8, illuminates how parents account for and move between discussions of assessment and documentation in offline and online contexts. The chapter also highlights both the constraints of documentation and how the discussions between parents online can be used as an arena to criticize documentalized practises and to empower parenthood. Both of the chapters in this section, on the one hand, challenge the common notion that parent–teacher collaboration always has positive effects and, on the other hand, show the importance and appreciation of home–school/ECE collaboration from the parental perspective.

7

THE GOVERNANCE AND THE PEDAGOGICALIZATION OF PARENTS

In the present-day education of children and young people, home–school collaboration is taken for granted, and parents are presumed to be involved in their child's education. In the report 'Starting Strong III' on early childhood education and care (ECEC), published by the OECD (Organization for Economic Co-operation and Development), this starting point is phrased in the following way: 'The involvement of parents in young children's education is a fundamental right and obligation /.../ ECEC services should recognise mothers' and fathers' right to be informed, comment on and participate in key decisions concerning their child' (OECD, 2012, p. 220).

Parental involvement in early education is encouraged, and the traditions of collaboration vary in different countries and educational systems. However, when involvement concerns the individual child, it is common for documentation to be deployed. In the Nordic context it would be difficult to imagine a parent–teacher meeting without some kind of documentation. As earlier chapters of this book have shown, discussions about children usually involve the use of specific documentation tools, for example, portfolios or individual educational plans (IEPs). Documentation can also be used as a way of stimulating interaction, for example, 'Strengths Cards' (see Chapter 6). In any case, assessment is either an explicit or implicit aspect of the collaboration.

In this chapter we take a closer look at parent–teacher collaboration in the contexts described above. We examine the position of the parent in 'documentalized' collaboration and critically discuss the demands that are placed on the parent. Again, we use empirical examples to elucidate our examination. The examples are based on our studies of parent–teacher meetings in Finnish and Swedish ECE. In our examination we apply the approach of governance (e.g. Miller & Rose, 2008; Rose, 1996a). That is, we consider ECE and its practices as an agent and as a technology (Rose, 1996a, pp. 26–7) in 'cultural reasoning' that produces discourses which regulate the lives of the children, parents and families (Bloch,

Holmlund, Moqvist & Popkewitz, 2003, p. 7). However, the approach of governance does not refer to the idea of a simplistic hierarchy of domination and subordination. Rather, the notion of power is linked to knowledge about human subjectivity. Power acts through practices that 'make up subjects as free persons' (Rose, 1999b, p. 95) and through the aspirations of subjects rather than in spite of them (Rose, 1996a, p. 155). This means that education, like other social institutions, is understood as a practice that encourages us to conduct our lives according to the desired objectives of society.

Our approach differs from that used in the mainstream studies of home–school, especially when it comes to ECE collaboration and parent involvement in education. In the following, we briefly present well-known and more recent and critical perspectives on these issues. We then move on to scrutinize governance by using empirical examples from parent–teacher meetings.

Perspectives on home–school collaboration

The impetus for underlining home–school cooperation is usually the notion of its beneficial and desirable effects on the child. There is an abundance of research that examines the associations between parental engagement in school and the child's well-being, development and learning (de Carvallho, 2001; Hallgarten, 2000). According to the common assumption – and many research findings – parents' involvement correlates positively with children's school achievements and social behaviour. The classic reference for these ideas is Bronfenbrenner's (1979) bio-ecological theory on human development (see also Bronfenbrenner & Morris, 2006). Bronfenbrenner argues for the importance of cooperation between the two main micro-systems involved in child development: family and school or ECE. Following his line of thinking, a lot of research has presented various functional ideas and models of home–school/ECE collaboration (e.g. Carr & Lee, 2012; Keyes, 2002; Kumpfer & Alvarado, 2003; Rose, 1999b).

Another frequently used model in research on home–school collaboration is Epstein's categorical description of parental involvement in education (Epstein, 1995). Epstein differentiates between parents who create a good and supportive learning environment at home, have a mutual communication with the school, participate directly in activities at the school and assist with homework, and parents who are actively involved in the governing of the school. Hanafin and Lynch (2002) describe similar roles in their analysis of the prevailing discourses on the home–school relationship. According to them, parents can be described as advocates for their children, consumers of education, partners and supporters. They can also be seen as problems, culture bearers, employees and learning entities (cf. Vincent, 1996; Hallgarten, 2000). Moreover, Ravn (2005) considers the home–school relation from the perspective of its rationales. She makes a difference between the pedagogical rationale which implies an educational partnership between the parties, the humanistic rationale that contributes to a democratic partnership, and an economic rationale that refers to a producer–consumer partnership.

Ravn's (2005) typology shows an increasingly common phenomenon in educational literature, which is that home–school collaboration and parental involvement are often discussed in terms of partnership (e.g. Alasuutari, 2010a; File, 2001; Foot, Howe, Cheyne, Terras & Rattray, 2002; Hughes & MacNaughton, 2000; Karila, 2006; Nichols & Jurvansuu, 2008; OECD, 2001, 2006, 2012; Tayler, 2006). In their analyses, Powell and Diamond (1995) show how early childhood programmes in the USA have developed from considering parents as learners to defining them as knowledgeable and collaborative partners. The same applies to the Nordic countries. The prevailing view during the construction of the welfare state and the expansion of ECE from the 1960s to the 1980s was that these services complemented the home (e.g. Välimäki & Rauhala, 2000). Parents were considered to be in need of help to support their children's development and education in a 'good or right' way (Popkewitz, 2003; Hendrick, 2004). Nowadays, the term cooperation or partnership is increasingly used in discussions about home–ECE relations (OECD, 2012). Furthermore, in the Finnish curriculum, partnership is described as forming the framework of parent–teacher collaboration (Stakes, 2004, p. 28), and in the Swedish Education Act (2010) the term cooperation is frequently used when referring to the relation between home and ECE centres.

In the literature on ECE, partnership is primarily portrayed as a positive, unproblematic and seemingly neutral concept (cf. OECD, 2012). However, a growing number of critical texts have been produced on the subject, as well as on home–school collaboration in general. Some researchers have questioned whether cooperation between home and school is always good, or whether it is good for all children and parents (Vincent & Martin, 2000; de Carvallho, 2001; Lahaye, Nimal & Couvreur, 2001). Hughes and MacNaughton (2000) argue that parents are constantly 'othered' in the literature on parental engagement, and that this leads to the subordination of parental knowledge to professional knowledge (cf. Borg & Mayo, 2001). Moreover, Vincent and Tomlinson (1997) state that partnership does not usually entail much more than parents' passive receipt of information. This is often the case if a parent has a lower level of education, social status or a minority background (Karlsen Baek, 2010; Lareau, 2000).

Much of the critical discussion is rooted in studies of power and governance (e.g. Rose, 1996a; Rose & Miller, 2008). It has been argued that even though partnership and the interlinked contractual nature of public services seem to emphasize the client's independence and equality in the client–official relationship, true equality can never be reached in the relationship; the contract merely disguises the existing power relations as a partnership (Sulkunen, 2007, 2009). Also, the notion of the history of partnership as an evolutionary story of broadening participation has been challenged. It has been stated that partnership reforms also link the governing patterns of the state to civil society and the principles of individual action (Franklin, Bloch & Popkewitz, 2003, pp. 5–6). Hence, the language of partnership is seen as an administrative, steering instrument that communicates expectations and demands to parents, and as a justifying mechanism which seeks to control parents and children (Borg & Mayo, 2001; Määttä & Kalliomaa-Puha, 2005; Strandell, 2011).

In general, education can be seen as 'a normality project' in modern society (Popkewitz, 2003, p. 55): 'Pedagogy is the inscription device of governing. Its intellectual techniques map the interior of the child and parents to render them visible and amenable to government' (ibid., p. 36). The ideal parent in the normality project is one who is involved in the construction of what is considered to be 'a good citizen'. Parents are expected to give the 'right' support so that children succeed and to share the ideas and preferences of the institution. Hence, the messages that emanate from research and from policy documents pedagogicalize parents: 'The successful parent is a pedagogical one' (Popkewitz, 2003, p. 51). In contrast, the construction of the good parent implicitly produces a less good parent with flaws, i.e., a parent who does not cooperate with the educational institutions in the right way, who has different preferences or requirements, or who criticizes taken-for-granted assumptions (Popkewitz, 2003; Rose, 1999b).

Critical studies on partnership and parent-school/ECE collaboration do not suggest that the regulation, governing and pedagogicalization of parents is explicit, but rather that these are typically implicit processes that occur in different collaboration practices and in/through the documents used in them (e.g. Markström, 2009). Parent–teacher discussions are one such example.

Parent–teacher meetings as a tool to govern parents

Parent–teacher meetings have been a common practice in Nordic ECE for decades, even though their aims and contents have varied contextually and changed over time. Nowadays, they are carried out in the spirit of educational partnership and with an emphasis on the individuality of the child (e.g. Lpfö98, 2010; Stakes, 2004). The meeting naturally focuses on the child, even though he/she is not usually present – at least when it comes to younger children. Instead, the adults discuss the child among themselves and, as previous research shows, usually focus on assessing the individual child regardless of whether this is the primary aim of the meeting or not (Alasuutari & Karila, 2010; Baker & Keogh, 1995; Markström, 2006, 2008, 2011a; Silverman, Baker & Keogh, 1998). It is also common for documentation to be deployed as a resource or support in the discussion. However, in these meetings it is not only the child, but also the parents who seem to become the target of auditing (Alasuutari, 2010b; Alasuutari & Karila, 2010; Alasuutari & Alasuutari, 2012; Karila & Alasuutari, 2012; Markström, 2011a, 2011b). In the following paragraphs we will present some empirical examples of this.

These empirical examples are based on studies carried out in the context of Swedish and Finnish ECE (e.g. Alasuutari, 2010b; Alasuutari & Alasuutari, 2012; Markström, 2005, 2008, 2010). The Swedish data concerns developmental talks (IDT) in 'preschools'. According to the national curriculum, such talks should be held at least once a year, with the aim of maintaining an ongoing dialogue with parents about the child's well-being, development and learning (Lpfö98, 2010, p. 13). In these talks, different institutional forms and documents are used as a point of departure. The Finnish data concerns parent–teacher meetings in which the parties draft an individual educational plan for the child (IEP). This is a regular practice in the country, in that each child in ECE is provided with an IEP (Stakes, 2004, pp. 29–30). Even though 'parent–teacher meeting' is used as an informative term for the IEP and IDT discussions, it is not entirely accurate, because the meeting is not just one-off incident, but a process that includes preparations, the actual encounter and its subsequent activities. In this chapter we focus on the preparations and the meeting itself, but not on the activities that follow. Table 7.1 describes the process as it has been carried out in the ECE centres participating in our studies. As can be seen from the table, the practices in Swedish preschools and Finnish ECE centres are similar, even though their main aims officially differ. The similarities are also evident in the techniques of governance, in which documentation practices play an essential role (see also Alasuutari & Markström, 2011).

Setting the scene

As can be seen from Table 7.1, the encounter between parents and teacher is preceded by a number of preparatory stages. Documents and documentation have an important function here. In addition to teachers collecting written and other material related to the children concerned, the parents and the children can also be involved in the preparations. Furthermore, the meetings are set and prepared in different forums: in everyday conversations between the teachers, in teacher conferences and potentially in the children's homes.

Based on our studies, the individual teachers are usually responsible for collecting information and other material for the forthcoming meeting. Observations of the child and written notes form part of their daily routines. They also collect the child's drawings and other artefacts that she or he has produced for use as resources in the meeting. Sometimes, teachers can also use premeditated or *ad hoc* testing to collect information about the child's skills and competences, for example, they can ask the child to write her or his name, draw a person, and name colours. This information can then be compared with the children's health care examinations undertaken to monitor their development and health. The results are then written down and reported to the parent in the meeting. Additionally, teachers can document what the child has said or done during the ECE activities.

Even though the individual teacher usually collects the material for the meeting, it is also common for the teachers to discuss the child prior to the meeting. This might occur in the midst of the hectic daily life of ECE, or the teachers may have a joint meeting in which they prepare for the coming talk with the parents and construct a joint view of the child. In the actual encounter with the parents, the individual teacher then conveys the 'corporate' view of the child, as in the following example, in which the topic of the talk is the child's language development:

TABLE 7.1 The encounters between parents and teachers as an ongoing process

	Finnish example *(Parent-teacher meetings in which the parties draft an Individual Educational Plan)*	Swedish example *(Individual Developmental talks in which documents/forms are often used)*
Preparations	A *local form* is used to structure the IEP discussion and comprises the actual IEP document. *The parent* is expected to fill out part of the IEP form at home. The parent is also expected to interview the child as instructed on the form. The parent should then take the form back to the institution. *The teachers* are expected to discuss the parent's answers, their views of the child and the issues they see as relevant for the child's IEP. They might also prepare by conducting observations and collecting material that exemplifies the activities of the class/child.	A *locally produced form* or questionnaire is often distributed to the teachers and the parents. *The parent* is expected to fill out the form at home. Parents are often expected to interview their child as instructed on the form. The parent then takes the form back to the institution. *The teachers* collect information from different sources about the child: from observations, colleagues, notes or documents, such as portfolios produced in ECE and notes from previous developmental talks. They might also fill out the same form as the parent, sometimes together with the actual child in preschool.
Meeting	Only the teacher(s) and the parent(s) are present. The discussion follows the topics and questions on the form. The IEP form is partly filled out in the meeting and signed by both parties. The teacher has a dominant position in the discussion. This means that she is in control of the interaction.	Only the teacher(s) and the parent(s) are present. The discussion follows the topics and questions on the form but can be used in different ways: the teacher first gives his/her picture (i.e. assessment) of the child, asks the parents to share their view of the child or do a comparison question by question. The teachers make notes during the discussions, which are then stored at the institutions, and only exceptionally (if there are any severe problems) write an action plan that should be signed by the parent. The teacher has a dominant position in the discussion, i.e. she is in control of the interaction.
After the meeting	The teachers are expected to discuss the IEP meetings in their team and thus, inform each other and discuss the individual plans of each child. The IEP should form the basis of the child's institutional education.	The notes and the documentation from the meetings (forms, notes from the talks etc.) are stored in a locked cabinet in the preschool. These documents can be used for different reasons in the everyday work and also be commented on at a later developmental talk/meeting. Portfolios or other documents used in the developmental talks are continuously used in everyday practice until the next meeting.

TEACHER: You are not like concerned about it, are you?
MOTHER: No, not really.
TEACHER: Yeah, and neither are we.

It is common for teachers to use the plural 'we' in their talk, and hence, 'bring in' the other professionals in the team. There seems to be an implicit norm that the teachers act as a collective, and enter the encounter with one institutional and professional 'voice' (cf. Mishler, 1984; Dahlberg, Moss & Pence, 1999; Markström, 2005, 2011b).

Another important part of the preparations is the 'agenda' for the meeting – a document or memo that lists what will be discussed with the parent(s). It can be composed by the teacher(s) in the ECE setting, as is often the case in Sweden. These agendas are also often based on specially prepared forms. In the Finnish data, a locally designed form serves as the agenda for the meeting in several ECE centres (see Alasuutari & Karila, 2010). The agenda often includes inquiries, or a short questionnaire for the parents to answer, the aim being to involve them in the assessment of their child and the evaluation of the institution.

In our studies, it was common for parents to receive the forms or the agenda prior to the meeting, so that they were informed about the topics in advance. Parents were sometimes also expected to fill out parts of the form before the meeting. Some of the questions on the form explicitly concerned their parenting, as will be shown in the next section. However, more often than not, the questions addressed the child's personality, development and interests. Even though these questions were mostly about the child, many of them could not be answered and discussed without references to parenting. For example, inquiries about the child's doings at home tacitly concern parenting and the activities that the parents offer and provide for the child. Consequently, the inquiries suggest normative ideas about parenting. A prime example is the seemingly innocuous and educationally well-grounded question about the child's favourite book that she/he wants to 'read' at home. Although this question is about the child, it also implies that it is natural or assumed that parents read to their children (and that children like to be read aloud to). Other questions concern watching TV, using other kinds of media and eating and sleeping habits at home. In Foucault's (1991) terms, these kinds of questions and talk can be labelled as 'pastoral power', i.e., a technique that can be used to govern and make people confess their shortcomings, and in this context entice the parent to admit to the teacher that she or he is not a perfect parent. This confession is the point of departure for self-governance.

In the questions and invitations to talk about parents' actions we can identify the norm of visibility of home and parenting, even though this is concealed in the 'child'-oriented nature of the questions. When parents prepare in the way that is expected of them – by reading the documents and answering the questions – they are made ready for the dissolution or blurriness of the limit between private and public. This blurriness seems to be an essential part of the relations in the intermediate domain between the home and the ECE centre (e.g. Alasuutari, 2010a; Forsberg, 2007; Mayall, 2002). As will be discussed later, the dissolution again allows for the application of various forms of governance in the parent–teacher interaction.

In some of the preschools involved in our study, parents were also expected to prepare for the meeting by discussing ECE with their child and by noting her or his views on a special form (see also Chapter 6). For example, the child might be asked to reflect on her- or himself, and on her or his behaviour and situation as a preschool child (cf. Dean, 1999; Donzelot, 1997; Rose, 1996a). In the meeting with the teacher, the parent was then expected to report the child's answers. In other words, the interaction and talk in the context of the home was documented and used in another social context, namely the developmental talk (Alasuutari, 2013; Markström, 2009).

According to our studies, the preparations for the parent–teacher meetings are essentially about documentation. They are important for setting the scene for the actual encounter and conveying what will be on the agenda. Hence, they indicate what the meeting will be about and what will be addressed in it. The 'documentalized' preparations also prescribe the dominant discourse(s) of the meeting, which are usually based on institutional and professional ideals and developmental psychology. Finally, they position the parties in a specific way by prescribing asymmetric power relations. The parent is mainly positioned as an interviewee (Karila & Alasuutari, 2012) and expected to be ready to discuss and disclose parenting issues and family life. In this way, the private is moved to the public sphere.

Governance in (inter)action

Based on our data, the atmosphere of parent–teacher meetings is usually informal and relaxed. The discussions are not as official as in many other forms of institutional interaction (Alasuutari, 2009; Markström, 2005). Also, the teachers often underline the informality of the discussions (Alasuutari, 2010a). However, as has already been suggested, parent–teacher meetings are not free from power issues and the governance function of ECE, despite their seemingly easy-going character and the commonly-assumed partnership between the parties (e.g. Stakes, 2004); Lpfö98, 2010; Skolverket, 2010). In reality, in the face-to-face meetings between parents and teachers, we can see how the assessment of the child, the advisory nature of the exchange and the monitoring of potential risks all serve to govern parents and parenting. This aptly exemplifies Ferraris' (2013) argument about documentality and documentation being the condition of governance. In the three-party interactions between the document, the teacher (as a professional) and the parent, the document contributes to the production of 'facts' and acts as a 'neutral agent'. In this way, documents participate in the transmission of ideals and models of behaving and being. Consider the following statements from four different teachers about different children:

Here I have written that she shows that she is happy and nice to her friends.

(Teacher A)

Yes, I have written that she is doing pretty well compared to the other children of her age.

(Teacher B)

I'll see (browses the documents), eh, about his understanding of words, I have written that he could answer the questions.

(Teacher C)

I have written that we all think he is much better now. There is a big difference compared to last year.

(Teacher D)

All the above statements indicate how the teachers have assessed the child. Our studies show that as written words, the statements seem to deal with and stand for something more than just a presentation of the individual teacher's or the teacher collective's (contextual) views and ideas about the child. The documentation somehow detaches the statements from the people who have made them and transforms them into external or objective 'facts'.[1] In other words, the written word seems to give special weight and authority to the statement. This aligns with what has been identified in studies of talk in other institutional contexts (e.g. Mäkitalo, 2005).

Even though the teachers' assessments in the above statements concern the child (the primary focus of the meeting), they also imply an assessment of the parent. As mentioned earlier, discussing the child also conveys notions about the parent, parenting and the parents' shortcomings. The parent is thus also assessed in the parent–teacher meetings. When the child is portrayed as an ordinary or a 'normal' child (see Chapter 5, also Markström, 2009, 2010; Alasuutari & Markström, 2011), the documentation suggests a positive appraisal of the parent (cf. Alanen, 2009). That is, it produces a parent who is doing proper parenting. When the child does not meet the 'criteria', expectations about parenting are often aired in the parent–teacher meetings, either implicitly or openly, as in the following example:

TEACHER: She really has a character that demands special limits. Like, she could surely make quite a mess if she just wanted to do that.
MOTHER: Uhum
TEACHER: So, well, just clear limits.

Here, the teacher's description of the child as having a 'character' that needs clear limits concludes a longer interaction episode in which the mother expresses her alignment with this kind of interpretation about her child. The co-constructed characterization of the child enables the teacher to conclude by making a suggestion about the relevant behaviour for a parent with such a child, namely to set 'clear limits'. The suggestion, which can also be understood as advice, is phrased in a way that makes it clear that it is aimed (also) at the parent.

In the previous example, the teacher's suggestion is based on talk about the child. Parenting is another topic of discussion that usually includes implicit or explicit advice, as illuminated in the next example. It starts with the teacher reading a question aloud from the IEP form about disagreements, which the parent has answered at home.

TEACHER: Ehm. How do you solve disagreements? (Reads the question from the form) Yeah, this is good this penalty bench.[2]
MOTHER: Yeah, it is in the kitchen and visible from everywhere.

After the teacher has read the question from the form there is a pause in the recording. During the pause she is presumably reading the mother's answer. In her response the mother describes the use of a penalty bench as a way of disciplining the child. The teacher then gives a positive appraisal of the disciplinary method, which at the same time includes encouraging feedback and an assessment of parenting practices.

The example illuminates how forms have the power to make delicate issues 'neutral'. In many countries, setting limits for a child is a popular topic and a concern in discussions about parenting. (Consider, for example, the popularity of programmes like 'Super Nanny'.) This topic can often be delicate in a parent–teacher meeting, because it can be understood as questioning parenting practices. Therefore, if no documentation has been deployed, presenting a question about setting limits for the child could require some interactional preparations – explanations or preparatory accounts – on the part of the teacher (cf. Linell & Bredmar, 1996; Peräkylä, 1995, pp. 232–86). When the topic is introduced via a form, it is detached from the teacher and seems more neutral. This finding can be conceptualized as a hybrid of human and nonhuman influences in which the form displays an agency by doing things that the humans alone could not do in the same way (Cooren, 2004; Latour, 1996).

In the two previous examples, the teacher suggests to the parent what he or she should do. Thus, both episodes exemplify advice giving and 'parent education', i.e., a pedagogicalization of the parent (Popkewitz, 2003). This is common in parent–teacher meetings, albeit indirectly. In addition, the parent education in the examples is intertwined with a monitoring of potential problems, risks in the family and parenting, which can also be understood as a specific governance technique.

In the two previous examples, the notion of potential risk deals with the disciplining of the child and is grounded in psychological discourse. Other kinds of risk monitoring can also be identified in our data. The questions about everyday care provide one opportunity for this. The following example lists the questions that the teacher poses to the mother of a two-year-old girl, Tina. Prior to the quoted questions the parties have been talking about Tina's eating habits at home and at day care; a topic that was introduced by the heading 'Eating' on the IEP form serving as the agenda for the meeting.

TEACHER: How is it, does Tina eat a lot of sweet stuff at home? Is she like that? (The mother gives a lengthy account and explains that the child is not given any sweets except on special occasions.)

TEACHER: Okay, what about, does Tina eat sweet snacks and so on more than regular meals? (The mother explains that the only sweet stuff that Tina is given is yoghurt and pureed fruit, but only as a dessert. According to her she likes them.)

TEACHER: That's very good. It's a good habit, so the child will learn that first you have the hot meal.

The teacher's questions address the child and position her as the agent with regard to her eating. At the same time they deal with issues that cannot be discussed separately from parenting, especially considering the age of the child. The questions thus monitor the parenting provided by assessing parental behaviour in relation to the child's nourishment. They also show how parent education is intertwined with the monitoring (cf. Popkewitz, 2003). The example illuminates governance with double or multiple functions: the assessment of parenting practices and the education of the parent to transmit proper thinking about eating and meals to the child, so that the child will internalize the right ideas and habits about preserving one's health. That is, the text, talk and interaction are to a large extent driven by what the child should be like from an educational perspective, and in relation to what is seen as a good preschool child (Alasuutari & Markström, 2011; Markström, 2011a, 2011b). This requires parents who are interested in, understand, embrace and share the pedagogical discourse, and consider their own children from the institutional perspective.

All the examples in this section show how the written text is used as a point of departure in the face-to-face encounter between the teacher and the parent. They also illuminate the intertwinement of text and talk in these meetings. The documents are not just tools, but play an important role in carrying out the 'project' assigned to the meeting, regardless of whether this is a developmental talk or an IEP (cf. Mäkitalo, 2005). While doing this, they also play an essential role in the governing of parents by facilitating the assessment and education of parents and the monitoring of potential risks in the family or parenting. What is documented is thereby detached from the professional actor(s), that is, from the teacher(s). Therefore, the assessment, which is intertwined with documentation, is transformed into an objective fact and the delicate topic into a seemingly neutral inquiry. This enables a parent–teacher interaction that seems to be smooth and easy-going, also with regard to sensitive and morally-laden issues.

Conclusion

The importance of cooperation and partnership between home and ECE centres for children's development and learning is underlined in different official documents, such as curricula, and underpinned in research literature. Our examination of the 'key' encounters between teachers and parents in Swedish and Finnish ECE – the talks about the child's development (IDT) and individual educational plan (IDP) – show how essentially the cooperation is intertwined with documentation. The preparation for and conduct of the meetings we examined were thoroughly documented and the documents were used or re-visited by the educators and/or the parents.

Parents and children are usually involved in the documentation practices, although it is primarily the teacher's task as a professional to be in charge of the 'documentalized' preparations for the meetings and to govern the conversations that arise in them. The documentation underlines the institutional character of the meetings and ensures that the parent–teacher interaction is to a large extent based on the terms of the ECE setting (Alasuutari, 2010b; Markström, 2011b). In the documentalized practices, parents are 'schooled' in the institutional dis-courses. This schooling forms an elementary aspect of their governance and pedagogicalization (Popkewitz, 2003). Through documentation, the parents are also made ready to 'render them(selves) visible and amenable to government' (Popkewitz, 2003, p. 36).

The focal person of the meeting and the utterances is the absent child, in that the documentation and the talk between the teacher and the parent are mostly about her or him. Consequently, the child is implicitly or explicitly assessed during the IDT and IEP meetings (e.g. Alasuutari & Karila, 2010; Baker & Keogh, 1995; Markström, 2006, 2009; Pillet-Shore, 2003). The parent is expected to participate in the assessment and to examine the child's strengths and short-comings. This joint assessment of the child presumes a parent who is interested and involved in the categorization of the child, and who embraces and shares the corresponding discourses of the institution – that is, the ideas about what a 'proper' child in ECE is like (see Chapter 6; Alasuutari & Markström, 2011; Markström, 2011a, 2011b).

However, the gaze on the child often entails an implicit appraisal of the parents' actions. Through documentation and the talk about the child, parents are invited to reflect on themselves and their parenting. At the same time, the documentalized practices imply standards of good parenting and a 'competent' or desirable parent from the point of view of the ECE setting, for example, a parent who is ready to answer the required questions (Alasuutari, 2013). This means that the practices also position the parent as a potential improvement project. For example, by specific questions and implicit advice given by the teachers, parents are pedagogicalized to give the 'right' kind of care and support to their child. This can also be interpreted as a pastoral technique and as self governance (Foucault, 2003) that constructs a subject that is rational and self monitoring. In the case of IDT and IEP talks, this is a parent who both corresponds and relates to the institutional notions of a desir-able ECE child (cf. Biesta, 2011).

Our data also reveals the intertwinement of the pedogogicalization of the par-ents and the surveillance of potential risks in child development and welfare. The IDT and IDP processes topicalize issues, such as disagreements between the parent and the child, which are then used as opportunities to implicitly educate the parent about the appropriate way of dealing with a situation. At the same time, the topics provide a possibility to assess and evaluate potential risks, for example, in parenting. These inquiries into the parent, the child and the family can be understood as echoing the increased public concern for children, and the emphasis on early intervention that has become more apparent in Western countries in recent decades (e.g. James & James, 2008; Parton, 2006, 2010, 2011; Satka & Harrikari, 2008). In short, they signal the emergence of a new form of governance and a regime of risk politics.

Notes

1   As Chapter 6 revealed, the power of the document to produce facts also depends on the assumed rights of knowing the person whose views have been registered. Consequently, the child's documented views can be challenged and disqualified by the adults.
2   Ice hockey is a very popular sport in the Nordic countries. The term 'penalty bench' in the example refers to the penalty box employed in ice hockey. The use of the penalty bench is often discussed in the Finnish parent–teacher meetings in our data.

8

PARENTHOOD BETWEEN OFFLINE AND ONLINE

About assessment and documentation

The previous three chapters have described in different ways how documentation is used to assess the child in parent–teacher talks and to involve the parent in this assessment. They have also illuminated the constraints of the parental position in these talks. In the meetings, the parents are primarily expected to align with and acquiesce in the institutional discourses and practices. Through guidance and advice, they seem also to be subjectified as the objects of pedagogicalization (see Popkewitz, 2003). In addition, the parents are positioned as the targets of (risk) assessment regarding their parenthood. All these findings can be linked with the principles of institutional interaction, which the parent–teacher meetings are, regardless of their potential informality and easy-going atmosphere (cf. Alasuutari, 2009; Markström, 2005). The interaction in them is guided and framed by the objectives of the meetings and ECE, and by the institutional positions of the parties as an expert and as a layperson (see Drew & Heritage, 1992). From this perspective it is also easy to understand why the parents do not often present any criticism of the practices in the discussions.[1]

In this chapter we will move out from the educational institutions and their constraints on parental talk. Instead, we will examine Internet sites where parents discuss among themselves documentation and assessment in educational institutions. As a research context, the Internet sites differ considerably from the institutions. Often they allow anonymity, as is the case in our research material, and are therefore more 'faceless' than the institutional encounters. Furthermore, they do not demand accountability in the same manner as face-to-face talks; each participant can just drop out of the discussion at any moment. Even though the new media, with its Internet sites, blogs and the social media, surrounds us all, it is still relatively little researched, particularly from a parental perspective (Vallberg-Roth, 2006, 2010).

As was discussed in the previous chapter, home–school relations have been examined a lot and bibliometric research shows an increase in the number of such studies over a forty-year period (Castelli & Pepe, 2008). The Internet studies are obviously a recent phenomenon in this research field. The greatest increase in these studies has taken place in the field of psychological research. A survey of psychosocial research – in the medical, educational and sociological disciplines – on parenthood and the Internet reveals an increased interest in this area since the end of the 1990s (Plantin & Danebeck, 2009). The research focuses on four main themes. During the early years, research was concerned with listing and analysing useful sites for parents. Later the studies started to pay more attention to the parents' usage patterns on the Internet. This was followed by studies that deal with activities in online support groups. In recent times, research has focused on questions concerning various interventions carried out via the Internet. The studies have also more often been geared to the parent–profession relation than to the parent–parent relation (Plantin & Danebeck, 2009).

In this chapter we will analyse and identify dimensions of parenthood in the intensified documentation and assessment practices, as they can be differentiated from the data taken from the Internet.[2] We use the term *intensified* to capture the denser documentation and assessment in all forms of communication, both non-electronic (offline) and electronic (online) communication (see Vallberg-Roth, 2012a). The data is drawn from two Swedish communities: 'Everything for parents – Your family on the net' ('Allt för föräldrar – Din familj på nätet') and 'Family life' ('Familjeliv'). In these online communities, it is possible for parents to discuss various topics and write about how they view the increasingly common assessment and documentation in ECE and school without jeopardizing their relations with the institution. We will analyse the currents of thought in these Internet discussions and examine the dimensions of parenthood that can be interpreted as intertwined with the intensified documentation and assessment practices. The analysis illuminates the complexity of contemporary parenthood between offline and online, and how parents can be both empowered and weakened in these communication practices.

Next we will present the findings of our analysis: four dimensions of parenthood that can be considered as embedded in interests concerning: the state; the market; evidence (scientific or pseudo-scientific); and the civil sphere. After presenting the dimensions of parenthood, we consider who assesses whom in the Internet discussions. The chapter ends with a discussion about transformative assessment between offline and online, and how parents seem to be both weakened and strengthened when they move between and operate in different dimensions.

Dimensions of parenthood: whose interests are involved?

Our analysis of the Internet discussions suggests that parenthood can be considered according to the dimensions of policy-related, evidence-related, market-oriented and civil-based parenthood. The complexity of interests involved in the different dimensions will be described below.

Policy-related parenthood

Many threads in our material relate to issues such as user influence and responsibility as well as increased communication and transparency between the home and ECE. Moreover, they can also reveal or consider power relations. Therefore, they can be characterized as policy-related currents of thought that have prominent claims to democracy, but that at the same time are framed or driven by state interests, which focus on home–school relationship and which are reflected in education policy. This dimension highlights the parents' position as citizens.

The dimension of policy-related parenthood is exemplified below through a few threads that concern increased information and transparency in school, and power relations and inequality in practices.

> I think it's (individual developmental plan, IDP) good. It gives both us parents and the child a possibility to know from the beginning what the child is good at and what we need to work a bit extra with.

> Anyway, I look forward to clear goals and clear statements as to how far my child has come in relation to the targets. No more woolly 'she's so good'.

> A good thing about grade-like written assessments from the very first year is that both teachers and parents see how the child's work and development are progressing.

> As it is today it's uneven in Sweden's schools how feedback to the home and students works as to how things are actually going in school.

As can be seen, the views concerning assessment and documentation in the Internet material are both positive and negative. There are appreciative appraisals of assessment and documentation practices, such as of IDP in the example. Moreover, assessment and documentation are valued, since they provide information to the parent about the child's progress.[3] However, the threads also present allusions to problems, like the one in the example concerning potential inequality regarding how schools provide feedback to homes and to the students.

The dimension of policy-related parenthood can be associated with a democratized parenthood – which also partly permeates the entire data – since it points out the parents' possibilities to make their voice heard, to obtain information, and to expose power relations through Internet environments. However, the question of increased information that is emphasized in education policy and underlined by the parents in the threads, can be problematized in relation to reciprocal communication. The emphasis on information and arguments concerning the duty of schools and teachers to inform the parents seem to have increased, thus disfavouring reciprocal dialogue and democratic communication (cf. Tveit, 2007). The notion of information can be associated with relatively one-sided communication in which, in the case of education policy, the standards are determined by the state (Kristofferson, 2008).

The problems of written communication are also pointed out in some of the threads of the discussions. Below is one example of them:

> How can a few lines on a sheet of paper be clearer than a conversation between children, parents and the teacher, where you have an opportunity to ask questions, discuss and together arrive at any problems that exist, strategies and targets?

This example relates not just to issues concerning functional communication but also to a more general question about the value and meaning that are given, on the one hand, to talk and, on the other hand, to written words. It can also be linked with the debates about 'contractualization' of home–school collaboration (Åkerstrøm-Andersson, 2003). As Chapters 6 and 7 have shown, parent–teacher collaboration is intensely based on documented communication and on the use of documents that can be in the end signed by the parties. This can be related to the tendency towards a reliance on contracts in the regulation and governance of parenthood (Åkerstrøm-Andersson, 2003). For example, the individual development plans can be regarded as contract-like documents since they regulate responsibilities and virtually always include the signatures of teachers, parents and students (Alasuutari & Karila, 2010; Asp-Onsjö, 2010; Vallberg-Roth & Månsson, 2009). There are also home–school contracts stating that the parents must show an interest in their children's education, must be interested in the children's homework, ensure that the children are well rested and have had breakfast, know what the children do in their spare time, check that they do not watch certain television programmes and go to bed in time (see Bartholdsson, 2007). Similar contracts can also be constructed in ECE centres/preschool, for instance, in action plans (Simonsson & Markström, 2013). As was discussed in the previous chapter, the 'contractual' collaboration is interlinked with the notion of partnership. On the one hand, they can be seen both as means of regulating and governing parents to fulfil the demands of desirable parenthood. On the other hand, they can comprise a tool for teachers to get support from the parents in their professional work (Simonsson & Markström, 2013).

While school, in a Nordic perspective, has been given increased control vis-à-vis the family through assessments, tests, contracts, etc., the family's influence vis-à-vis the ECE has increased, based on principles of equality and democratization, at least in the rhetoric (cf. Persson & Tallberg Broman, 2002). Both of these aspects are also reflected in the dimension of policy-related parenthood.

Evidence-related parenthood

Part of the Internet discussions we have studied can also be described as reflecting an aim at evidence-related parenthood, which seeks knowledge and grounds parenthood on tests, parental education, standardized assessment and documentation (cf. Biesta, 2007; Grimen, 2009; Thomas & Pring, 2004). The evidence-related dimension is characterized by an interest in and a claim to knowledge, and deals with professionalization of parents on a scientific basis. In this dimension parents can be viewed as scientific and evidence-based actors.

Previous research shows that parents can be highly involved in their children's life and simultaneously self-critical (cf. Alasuutari, 2010b; Forsberg, 2009; Markström, 2010). Uncertainty, confusion, and the ambition to be perfect and to get evidence that one is doing right and being successful seem to motivate parents in some of their Internet discussions. Documentation in this context can be viewed as evidence, that is, as systematically documented data with a scientific base and connection. The dimension of evidence-related parenthood can be exemplified through the following Internet communication about standardized assessment instruments:

> Hi, Our daughter is in pre-school class and has been able to read for a year or so /.../ They assess the children's reading ability in pre-school but nothing that is documented as when they start school. Do you other parents who have children in pre-school know about your children's learning in school and are you also curious?

> Borrow the book about the Reading Development Scheme from the library. It's easy to check for yourself.

> I have heard that there is some type of colour circle (TRAS) where you colour different segments and as the child develops there is more colour in the segments. I have only just heard about this circle and I think it sounds good. Anyone who knows?

Questions can be raised about whether evidence-based practice helps to empower and increase confidence or to disempower and weaken confidence in parenthood. Gustavsson (2010) says that he has noticed a tendency for uncertainty among parents to increase in pace with the growth of expert advice (cf. Vandenbroeck, Roets & Snoeck, 2009). He says that he himself as an expert has probably also contributed to this. Grimen (2009) examines evidence-based professional practice and problematizes the relationship between expert rule and democracy. He is sceptical about the democratization argument, which he thinks is based on premises that are not especially plausible (cf. Biesta, 2007). For example, members of the public can click their way into databases to read surveys of knowledge, but they find it difficult to evaluate the quality of these summaries. Evidence-related parenthood that can lead to embedding of the parent–child relationship in tests and standards suggests an instrumental and manual-based parenthood that needs further research. What does it mean for children, for example, if they are also tested and diagnosed by the parents in the home?

Market-oriented parenthood

Furthermore, a market-oriented parenthood can be detected in the material studied. Market-oriented parenthood is about being seen, noticed, talked about and desirable. Here the quest to be seen and chosen is the distinctive feature, for example, through exposure to commercial sites. Babies become web-babies and parents plan, discuss, expose, and can be said to market parenthood via the Internet. Parents and children can be regarded as consumers in an overall knowledge economy; parenthood simply follows the commandments to buy–sell–choose. Profiling oneself is a distinct trend arising under the influence of a worldwide, market-oriented ideology. It becomes crucial to be seen and profile oneself in the race to be chosen. Attracting attention, being spoken about, being desirable – these make up the foundation of consumer society (Bauman, 2007). A quest for assessment through documentation can be interpreted as compatible with today's life of consumption. Market- oriented parenthood can be illustrated with the following extracts from the analysed material:

PARENT 1: Today Anna's assessment arrived by post, I eagerly tore open the envelope and saw that she had met the goals in all the subjects. Of course I was pleased, but when I read on I became even more pleased. Anna is an orderly, good, and nice girl and she helps her classmates. Wonderful!

PARENT 2: How marvellous! But with a mother like that she could hardly be anything else.

PARENT 3: Oh, how nice ☺. It makes you happy as Larry to hear that other people also understand how wonderful your children are! But listen, – I checked your blog and liked your necklace! ☺ Do you make them and sell them?

There are different sides of the drive to be seen and chosen. Certain intentions and phenomena that are emphasized in policy and steering documents on different levels, such as the importance of children's right to be seen, heard and met, come together and seem to strengthen the market and media forces. In this way one could say that some of the democratic and market-oriented dimensions merge and can be difficult to identify and trace.

To understand the forces behind family consumption, the sociologist Allison Pugh (2009) spent a few years observing and interviewing children and parents in the USA. Pugh noted that children's desires derived less from striving for status or falling victim to advertising than from their longing to join the conversation at school or in the neighbourhood. Most parents react to children's needs for belonging by buying certain products and experiences that serve as passports into the children's social worlds, because they sympathize with the children's fear of being left outside or regarded as different from their peers. The family gives priority to children's wishes even during financial constraints. Pugh illustrates a surprising similarity of the fears and hopes held by parents and children from very different social contexts. So while corporate marketing comes into play in the commercialization of childhood, what really matters is a desire to belong. Perhaps the extracts above can also be interpreted as an outcome of a desire for belonging, through interplay between paying attention to successful parenthood and the interest in buying a necklace. Parents can be interpreted as floating between being supporting fellows and consumers.

Civil-based parenthood

Two types of currents of thoughts comprise the dimension of parenthood that we have linked to the civil sphere: the threads that approach the other members of the site as a collective, and discussions implying resistance or doubt about the educational practices and the professional. In this dimension of civil-based parenthood, parents mostly seek support via other parents on the Internet and exchange experiences with each other (cf. Plantin & Danebeck, 2009). Parents are then viewed as fellows. This can be exemplified with the following statements:

> Not needing to be totally dependent on someone else's guidance is always good, surely. Today the information is more accessible than in the past, when there was mostly someone who 'guarded' the information and brought it out for anyone who asked to share it. Today you can find an incredible amount on the Internet if you just know how to search.

> Now I'm sitting here with a questionnaire, an IDP [Individual Development Plan], but my head's stopped working. I can't think of a good answer to the questions in the form. Can I have some help? /.../ I'm really bad at this kind of thing and feel so STUPID about not being able to answer.

Both of the above examples refer to the Internet as a space or community that is outside the institutions, as the civil sphere. In the first one it is a site of information that frees the parent from being dependant on those (professionals) who have previously guarded the delivery of information. In the latter example the Internet provides a space for discussions among peers in a community that is bound together by the civil sphere (cf. Alexander, 2006; Trondman, Lund & Mast, 2011).

However, some threads also express doubt about the documentation practices and about teachers as professionals:

> I wonder what and how you get informed about your children in individual development talks?

> Sure, it's nice that children learn letters and numbers, but you shouldn't make great demands of small children. And IDP (Individual Developmental Plan) is a real FLOP.

Daun (1997) argues that the civil sphere tends to develop resistance against the other spheres of government and the market. 'Among the teachers, it can be manifested as resistance to the central directives and among parents and students it can be manifested as resistance to the culture that is produced and reproduced in schools' (Daun, 1997, p. 177). In the examples above, this resistance targets in concrete terms the individual development plans, which can be considered as reflecting the resistance of the educational system and its documentation practices in the policy-related dimension (resistance against government).

The dimension of civil-experience-based parenthood reflects a liberating and supportive potential between parents. Furthermore, it illustrates something of a confessional and (self) assessing function (cf. Fejes & Dahlstedt, 2012; Foucault, 1991). The involved and (self) critical parent stands out. This dimension displays features of a show-and-tell culture, or in other words public confessions, which the sociologist Bauman (2007) claims is a characteristic of fluid modernity. Transparency (cf. Brin, 2006), both social and mental nakedness, is what counts.

When it comes to who is assessing whom, there are examples of parents' utterances of teachers assessing children and examples of parents assessing teachers, children, other parents and themselves (see also Chapter 4). The following is a clear example where a parent in the network assesses the teacher and the teacher's assessment:

> You don't have to have met that teacher to write back with a written assessment: Unpedagogical and tactless. Lack of empathy and difficulty in putting across criticism in a constructive way.

Concluding comments

The complexities of contemporary parenthood in intensified documentation and assessment practices have been exemplified in this chapter through an analysis of the currents of thoughts on two Internet sites. In their discussions, the parents seem to move between offline and online, and they also operate in different dimensions: at a macro level related to policy, science and evidence, the market and the civil sphere. When the parents operate and move across the boundaries of these dimensions, they may also be viewed as actors in transition, in the sense of being either citizens, science-based actors, consumers or fellows.

Furthermore, the material presents the parent that differentiates between expert knowledge and experience-based knowledge. The former is now more easily available for the parent than previously. Professionalized parenthood on a scientific basis can be interpreted to be compatible with knowledge-intensive society, where the production of knowledge is the most important factor for growth and competitiveness.

In the complex dimensions of parenthood, on the whole we can see demanding, conflicting (conflicting views to consider parenting) and supporting parenthood (advice between parents as fellows in network). Demanding parenthood is shown between offline and online, both in the sense of time-consuming activities and in the sense that different views are exposed and spread in the network, based on experience, science, policy and/or the market and economy. As has been shown, these views may be conflicting, or consistent and supporting. They may empower and increase confidence and influence, or disempower and weaken confidence and influence in parenthood.

Moreover, we can see clear examples of added and transformed assessment in the communication through boundary-crossing flows. We have, for example, the Reading Development Scheme (LUS) which is introduced in the preschool institution (offline) and is then communicated electronically and flows in the home as parents encourage each other to test and document their children for themselves. Other examples show that assessment of children offline leads to assessment of teachers online (see also Chapter 4). The examples are based on the non-electronic individual development talk in ECE or school. The teacher's assessment of the child offline is transformed to parent's assessment of the teacher's assessment online.

Other examples (also in Chapters 4 and 7) show that assessment of children can lead to assessment of parenthood. A positive assessment of the child offline is communicated online by the parent. Additional and transformed assessment is illustrated by the way in which other parents assess and praise another person's parenthood.

The study presented in this chapter shows that parents create meaning by using a multitude of different forms of communication (see also Vallberg-Roth, 2012a; cf. Kress, 2003). In our time it can be interpreted as concerning challenging parenthood in communication- and knowledge-intensive consumer society. These currents of thought and dimensions of parenthood expose power relations and show, on the one hand, how the documentation and assessment practice can strengthen and empower, and on the other hand how it can weaken and restrict parenthood (cf. Steyerl, 2003). Furthermore, the currents of thought reveal how parents develop strategies, to adapt to, and express appreciation for, or opposition to the documentation and assessment practices.

Finally, the material illustrates the Internet as a channel for criticism, which we do not hear much in our studies of parent–teacher interaction in ECE. The question is, in which ways the criticism (as parental assessment of education) is functional. Is it followed; is the 'point taken' by the educational institutions?

Notes

1   Being critical of the institutional practices in the parent–teacher meetings would compromise the parents 'face' (see Goffman, 1967) as a collaborative partner. For example, in our Finnish data set of parent–teacher meetings, the parents criticize the documents that are used in them only if the teacher explicitly asks about their views or, first, expresses criticisms of the documents herself. In research interviews, the parents talk about the documentation and assessment more critically (e.g. Alasuutari, 2010b), but the interviews also suggest that parents primarily appreciate the parent–teacher meetings very much. Besides, it is very common that the parents, especially, want to learn about teachers' views and assessment of the child:

> I only have experience of one four-year-old, but the teachers have met dozens of them. It is always interesting to take part in their perceptions of our Karl. How is he in preschool. We know how he is at home but not how he is when we are not present. Does he play with the other children, does he have any friends and does he follow other four-year-olds in his development. That's what I expect to hear more about in the meetings.

Hence, in accordance with the institutional discourses and practices, the parents expect the teachers to assess their child and are mainly positive and curious about the teachers' views and findings. However, a research interview can also be seen as a form of institutional interaction. It serves specific objects defined by the researcher, whose position can be considered akin to that of a 'professional' in other institutional settings. The interviewee, again, is usually in the position of a layperson (see Drew & Heritage, 1992). Even though the research interviews that we have carried out give a somewhat different picture of the parent–teacher talks than the analysis of their interaction, it would be problematic to conclude that, for example, the interviews would give more accurate information about parents' position and views than the analysis of the interaction. Instead, we can only conclude that they provide us with different perspectives on the collaboration, as does the analysis of the Internet discussions in this chapter.

2   The chapter is mainly based on the article Vallberg Roth (2012a).
3   The parents' appreciation of the information provided by assessment and documentation can also be interpreted from the perspective of pedagogicalization (Popkewitz, 2003). When the parents underline the importance of the assessments as a foundation for their decisions about how to support the child they also show that they live by the idea of pedagogic parenthood conveyed to them in home–school collaboration and in education policy.

PART IV

Conclusion

9

DILEMMAS OF ASSESSMENT AND DOCUMENTATION

Below, is a quotation from a letter that a teacher (and a mother) sent to one of the authors of this book after reading her interview in a teachers' magazine. In the letter, the teacher told about her four-year-old goddaughter who had expressed her irritation about the daily 'report' that the educators of her early childhood education (ECE) centre had written to her parents. The goddaughter had said that the description of her peer relations was false. The discussion that the teacher had with her goddaughter and the interview she read made her present the following questions:

> I wonder why we document a child's peer relations and emotions and hence, define the child. How do we justify it? As an adult – for example, as a teacher like myself – I would not like to get a note from the headmaster to be taken to my family at the end of the day telling that I have discussed eagerly with Rita, the Swedish teacher; but I have been avoiding Peter, the gymnastics teacher, who is a bachelor, since he has a crush on me; or that I have been sitting at different lunch table from Margot, as I have not been getting along with her after she got the position I applied for; or that I have been really down because of my recent divorce or glowing with happiness after just becoming a grandmother.

When we have presented this quotation in workshops and seminars for teachers, scholars or students it has always made the audience laugh. Twisting the picture of the adult's role in the documentation practices has been taken as a joke and as a humorous story. This reveals how obvious the documentation of a child is for us, as educators and adults.

Indeed, documentation is seen as important, necessary and natural in ECE because of its links with the notions of the quality of early education. This link is emphasized at all levels of management and steering of ECE, which is also exemplified in the following quotation from the report 'Starting Strong II':

> Operational quality /.../ includes regular planning at centre and classroom level /.../ time allowed for child observation, assessments and documentation.
> *(OECD, 2006, p. 128)*

In her letter, the teacher dared to challenge the naturalized assumptions about assessment and documentation. She pointed at the observation, auditing and reporting of children's peer relations and the (assumed) experiences associated with them and posed a deeply ethical question: why do we think that we have the right to do this to children?

On the one hand, the dilemma that she presented can be related to Woodhead's (2005) argumentation. He proposes that it would be misleading to conclude that any single pattern of nurturance, care and education is an essential pre-requisite for children's healthy development. Consequently, child documentation could be deemed as a cultural choice and practice that is by no means necessary for children's well-being and development.

On the other hand, the dilemma presented by the teacher can also be associated with Ferraris' (2013) arguments about institutions and bureaucracy. According to him, institutional objects and institutions are constructed by documents, which therefore have an indispensable role in bureaucracy. This means that documentation is essential to bring into existence such things as learning, educator, the ECE child and the early education institution as a whole. Thus, it seems that we are left in between a rock and a hard place here. When we document the child, we are always dealing with values and, consequently, with a multitude of dilemmas. At the same time, an ECE institution without documentation appears to be an unfeasible prospect.

As the previous chapters of this book have shown, documentation in ECE applies different tools, comprises various forms of assessment, has different aims, fulfils several functions, and involves agents and influences from different levels and sectors of social life – not just children, parents and educators, but also actors and agencies at the national and international level. The chapters of this book have also highlighted that, even when the focus is on documents and documentation, we cannot totally dismiss interaction. The documents achieve their agency in interaction and social practices. This means that their agency is dependent on human agency. Therefore, text and talk are entangled in the documentalized practices of ECE.

In this concluding chapter we will outline the main points that we have discussed in the previous chapters and discuss contradictions and dilemmas in child documentation. First, we will consider ECE documentation from the perspective of the child and childhood and discuss, for instance, the tensions between the normative tendencies of education and the aims of individualizing education through documentation. Then we move on to examine the parents' position in child documentation and point out the duality of this position. We will also ask if it is the homogeneous or heterogeneous parent who is assumed to be involved in the documentation. In latter part of the chapter, we will consider the multidimensional steering of ECE documentation at the macro level; for example, what dimensions of global society are influencing and inter-twined with ECE documentation. All of these three sections are in different ways related to the educators' work. However, in the end we still consider documentation and its dilemmas from the viewpoint of the educators who carry the main responsibility for documentation in ECE.

The documentalized child and childhood

In the Nordic countries children's attendance at ECE is very high. This institu-tionalization of early childhood (e.g. Kampmann, 2004; Qvortrup, 2012) has also resulted in the regular assessment and documentation of the child from an early age. Previous chapters have illuminated the intensity of this documentation and indicated that the tools and practices of assessment and documentation can be more multiple and broader in their scope than the Nordic curricula on ECE sug-gest. Therefore, we can talk about multi-documentation in the Nordic ECE.

Based on Ferraris' (2013) thinking, we propose that this multi-documentation constructs social objects: this means that it brings different aspects of our social reality into existence. For example, different assessment and documentation prac-tices and tools are founded on various premises of the child and childhood, although these premises are not often made explicit or consciously pondered in the daily life of ECE.[1] Consequently, different assessment and documentation practices and tools often depict and construct a 'different' child. Some docu-mentation considers the child as an object that can be grasped and known by the educator through the assessment and documentation practices. Some take the child as a participating subject and as a human being with a voice that needs to be listened to. In short, the assessment and documentation that is used in ECE can be – and often is – based on contradictory notions and understandings of the child. The educator can be confronted with the question of what to make of these different pictures. For example, how can she rationalize the situation described in the letter that was presented in the beginning of this chapter? How should she relate to the report of the child's peer relations written by the staff and to the child's views of the report and of her peer relations that contradict the report? When answering this dilemma, the educator is dealing with a pro-found question about the idea of human being (and of the child as a human being). As has been shown in the book, sometimes answers can deploy, for instance, notions of traditional generational ordering, which give dominance to the adult view.

Commonly, motivations for child documentation are based upon perceptions that it produces something good for the child. This often entails that the documen-tation emphasizes the individual child and it is linked with the idea of individualized institutional education (cf. Kampmann, 2004; Strandell, 2011). For example, a child's language abilities are assessed with the objective of using the results in designing her or his early education in the best possible way, and hence to support her or him in acquiring adequate language skills. Nevertheless, the assessment of the child's abilities uses some criteria: a particular number of right responses or 'points' is defined as adequate language skills and the results below this are considered as deficiency. Therefore, the ideas about the individualization of institutional education – strived for with the help of documentation – are still tied up with the premises of assessment and documentation. Individualization is aimed at by comparing the assessed and documented child to some criteria of the 'average', 'ordinary' or 'normal'. Consequently, the educator is faced with the dilemma of standardization and homogenization within individualization (cf. Gitz-Johansen, 2004; Vallberg-Roth & Månsson, 2009).

In this book we have described the homogenization or 'normalization' of children as it is reflected, principally, in open forms of documentation and assessment in the parent–teacher talks. The expectations and norms of the ordinary child in our studies – that emphasize the child's sociability, play and peer relations and imply particular gendering – can be considered as the standards of the dominant culture, since our data concern primarily the majority population in Finland and Sweden (see Alasuutari & Markström, 2011). Based on our findings, we cannot say whether the same norms would frame the open forms of documentation of children with minority backgrounds. However, previous research on education suggests that the norms of the white middle-class usually predominate (e.g. Hosp & Reschly, 2004; Lappalainen, 2004). Consequently, there is a specific risk embedded in assessment and documentation: they can operate as a tool for both inclusion and exclusion of particular groups, characteristics, behaviours and individuals (Bundgaard & Gullov, 2008; Dahlberg, Moss & Pence, 2007; Gitz-Johansen, 2004; Popkewitz, 2008).

The dilemma of limited inclusion and specific exclusion does not only concern open tools of assessment and documentation. The more standardized means also have particular starting points and criteria and, therefore, they are intertwined with the contestation of how the reality (of learning, childhood, competences, etc.) may be constructed. In all, assessment and documentation in ECE are intertwined and consequential to what is seen as preferred and desirable for the children within the institution and as a social category in general. Therefore, they also embody a risk that the complexity of and diversity in childhoods may be neglected (cf. Vandenbroeck & Bouverne-De Bie, 2006).

Eventually, multi-documentation in ECE can be considered as part of the regulation and governance of present-day children (and parents and teachers), irrespective of its forms, means and aims (cf. Miller & Rose, 2008; Rose, 1999a). As a technology of governance (Rose, 1996a, pp. 26–7), multi-documentation of ECE is part of and produces a documentalized childhood; this means that childhood and the child are essentially delineated, defined and produced in and by documentation. Moreover, multi-documentation is a product of the 'adult' society – its traditions, cultural practices, and various discourses and trends. From the adult perspective, it is also easy to see that assessment and documentation can function as a support, for example, to parents in raising their child or to a teacher in designing her teaching in a more child-centred way. (For further information on complexity of the concept, see e.g. James, 2012.) However, with assessment and documentation, we have the same problem as with the institutionalization of early childhood in general: we know very little about what children think about it (cf. Qvortrup, 2012, p. 243).

Trondman's (2011) study, which is based on conversations with 40 children, aged four to six, makes us question whether documentation and assessment are what the children expect from ECE. Trondman concludes that from the children's perspective teachers are good if they are nice. A nice teacher is further characterized as responsible, caring, fair, empathic and interactively present. In her research concerning the documentation practices of a similar ECE setting to the one in which Trondman did his study, Vallborg-Roth (2011a, 2012b) concludes that the documentation did not primarily focus on caring or an interactive presence of the teacher, but on the requirements of the child's performance. Hence, the children did not seem to call for this kind of documentation, nor did they express the opinion that a nice teacher is a teacher who documents what the children are doing.

Ethnographic fieldwork also reveals that children do not always want to be registered. For example, when Ann-Marie Markström (2005) was doing her fieldwork and wrote down her observations of children's everyday activities in an ECE centre, some of the children wanted to know what she was doing and 'read' what she had written. Some children also clearly opposed the documentation. For instance, in one case two girls started to observe Ann-Marie and take notes on her. This example illuminates the same ethical dilemma as the letter at the beginning of this chapter: do we have the right to observe and document children or from where do we get this right (cf. Lindgren & Sparrman, 2003). From another angle we can ask whether (we want) children (to) learn that documentation is inevitable and one cannot say no to it.

Documentation with or on parents

While the institutionalization of children and childhood has been expanded to early childhood, the responsibility for child rearing and education has become more and more a shared task of the family and the state. Consequently, an increased emphasis and attention has been paid to home–ECE/school collaboration (Franklin, Bloch & Popkewitz, 2003; Vyverman & Vettenburg, 2009). The aspirations and demands of this cooperation are embodied in curricula and in different official documents both at national and transnational levels (e.g. Lpfö98, 2010; OECD, 2001, 2006, 2012). The point of departure is usually that the parents should (be able to) have continuous contact with ECE and that they should be motivated to collaborate in different ways. These demands are often justified by referring to the research showing that good relations between home and ECE institutions benefits children's development, well-being and lifelong learning (de Caravallho, 2001; Hallgarten, 2000). Recently, the debates have also drawn from more general discussions on parental rights to participate in and influence ECE institutions (OECD, 2012; Sandberg & Vourinen, 2007). This is something that can be linked to global discourses of democracy in modern society. The ideas and principles of, for example, pedagogical documentation resonate with these discourses. In addition, as a consequence of political and ideological tendencies to evaluate and audit educational institutions by, for example, ranking schools in a competing order, parental involvement has become more important (Englund, 2010).

In our studies we have been faced with the everyday reality that, whatever the impetus for parental collaboration is, it usually includes documentation. However, it seems that the parents often find themselves in a similar situation as the children in these documentalized practices: they are not really asked if they want to be involved in the practices or whether they would rather have a non-registered collaboration. This means that the parents cannot be considered as having anything like a 'consumer' relationship to these practices (see Hasenfeld, Rafferty & Zald, 1987): it is not possible for them to select and define what (documentation) services to 'buy' and what to discard.

However, the ECE institutions are also interested in parents' views, which is seen, for example, in the use of different feedback forms and questionnaires. As a documentation practice they position the parent close to a 'mode' that can be called a 'customer' (see Hasenfeld et al., 1987). It means that there is a consultation or negotiation with the customer about the services, to amend them to fit the customer's needs and expectations. It is documentation that makes the institution 'transparent' for the parents: by opening it to their evaluation by informing then about its functioning, the ECE institution can also be understood as approaching the parents from a customer perspective. Moreover, the parents are positioned as customers, for example, in the ideas of the Finnish IEPs, which should be based on a joint negotiation between the parent and the teacher about the child's early education (see Stakes, 2004, p. 29). However, in practice the picture is not so simple (e.g. Alasuutari, 2010b).

Although we can recognize some market-orientation in Nordic early childhood education, the parental position in the services cannot really be compared to that of a consumer or customer. Instead, the parents can be principally conceptualized as clients in the (documentalized) collaboration practices of present-day Nordic ECE (see Hasenfeld et al., 1987; Juhila, 2003). In short, the client mode refers to a position in which the parents have little control over the organizational rules and systems of the ECE institution and they are mainly expected to acquiesce in them. Documentation is an institutional practice and the parents are invited to participate in it according to the pre-defined institutional schemes. For instance, they can be expected to fill out specific parts of the documents and to interview their child following a set of questions. This often entails that the parents adjust to the institutional discourse – commonly based on developmental psychology – as we have discussed in this book.

Moreover, the parents are expected to participate in the assessment of their child. The assessment is usually embedded in the joint use of text and talk and seen as 'information exchange'. As the adults who know their child best (OECD, 2001, p. 117), the parents are expected to describe and characterize their child's behaviour, strengths, shortcomings and needs in different matters. They are also informed about the professionals' views of the child (that is, their assessments). These assessments can be used to direct the child's early education, but commonly they are also used as a resource in advising and guiding parents in their parenthood. In other words, the assessment and documentation transcends and blurs the boundaries between the home (private) and the institution (public), and they comprise the basis of the pedagogicalization of the parents (Popkewitz, 2003). Furthermore, documentation can be deployed in assessing such risks in child development that can be associated with parenting. Eventually, parents become the object of examination, categorization and government in the documentalized practices (Miller & Rose, 2008, Rose, 1996a).

All the different positions offered, suggested or imposed upon parents – from a customer to a client and from a subject and to the object of the documentalized practices – can be active at the same time. In our data on parent–teacher meetings – about the documentalized practices in action – we can see that the parents principally assume the position of a client and acquiesce in being an object of assessment. When being out of the institutional context of ECE – that is, in research interviews or in anonymous Internet discussions – they can also take a more critical stance to the practices.

Nevertheless, it is evident that to participate in and take an active position in the documentalized collaboration assumes that parents are skilled, interested and prepared to work together with the professionals and their children to manage the task of assessment and documentation. Consequently, the practices yield unspoken expectations and demands on parents about how to meet society's norms of good parenting and how to provide appropriate support for their child in lifelong learning. The notions of the 'good' parent also implicitly produce a picture of a less good parent with her or his shortcomings; this means, a parent who does not cooperate with the institution in the right way and who has different preferences than the institution and its professionals (e.g. Alasuutari, 2010a). Furthermore, the expectations commonly picture the parents as a homogeneous group.

The notion of parents as a homogeneous group makes parents from minority groups invisible and dismisses factors, such as class and ethnicity, that can play a crucial role in how parents understand home–school cooperation and act regarding it (cf. Crozier & Davies, 2007; Hanafin & Lynch, 2002; Vallberg-Roth & Månssson, 2009). There are differences in how parents from different backgrounds interact with teachers and the ECE institution due to social or cultural capital (cf. Karlsen Baek, 2010; Symeou, 2007). Middle-class parents are often equipped with the necessary cultural capital, use the same language as teachers, have knowledge about the education system and also expect that it is possible to influence the school and see themselves as able to have a say (cf. Borg & Mayo, 2001; Ball, 2006; Crozier et al., 2008). Furthermore, the teacher's values often correspond with well-educated and middle-class parents, rather than parents from lower socio-economic groups who are often less educated. Disadvantaged groups are often not familiar with or do not have the same resources to meet the educational system, its practices and the professionals. Therefore, it also is more likely that they, as parents, are often encouraged to be recipients of information rather than being urged to be involved in decision-making processes (Karlsen Baek, 2010).

In all, the examination of the documentalized home–ECE collaboration challenges the ideals of (equal) partnership in ECE. The relationship between the parties usually seems to be asymmetric and it emphasizes the teacher's and the institutions primary role in defining how the collaboration is carried out (e.g. Hughes & MacNaughton, 2000; Vincent & Tomlinson, 1997). Moreover, the children's homes and educational institutions usually have different resources in their collaboration, and they sometimes have different or even contradictory interests in it (although these are not necessarily explicitly stated) (Markström & Simonsson, 2013). Consequently, as partners in documentalized ECE practices, the parents seem to (be made to) follow the institution's lead.

Documentation and assessment from the institutional and professional perspective

The multi-documentation of ECE is steered, guided and influenced by a variety of factors. It is possible to differentiate micro-level aspects, for example, the specialization of the staff or the cultural background of the children, as having an effect on the choices and decisions concerning assessment and documentation in a particular institution. Similarly, the meso-level aspects, for instance, the local collaboration between welfare and educational services, guide the assessment and documentation in the ECE institutions. Furthermore, assessment and documentation is reflected in and is intertwined with the macro-level aspects and phenomena. These can be described as the conjunction of both national and transnational discourses and effects that are part of and construct a documentalized childhood. Macro-level aspects can be divided into policy-related, evidence-related, market-oriented and civil-oriented areas or dimensions. In steering and guiding multi-documentation, they reflect the interests of different actors and agents and comprise a whole that includes binding regulations, self-regulation and relational guiding through different mediums (Vallberg-Roth, 2013b). Although the dimensions can be seen as separate, they also overlap and are in practice somewhat difficult to identify. Furthermore, they are neither consistent nor coherent within or between themselves.

The policy-related area of the steering of ECE documentation concerns the dimension of democratic rights and obligations that are usually state-controlled (in de-/re-centralized steering), but which also reflect transnational influences.

Transnational trends and ideas are often based on or draw from comparative investigations that reflect neo-liberal thinking (Alasuutari & Qadir, forthcoming). In them, early education is commonly considered as an investment in the future, which is again phrased in terms of quality in the educational literature.

As an example of transnational trends, it is possible to recognize a tendency to the harmonization of and an adaptation of Nordic ECE policies at a national level in line with the suggestions of different OECD projects (cf. Alasuutari & Alasuutari, 2012; OECD, 2001; e.g. OECD, 2006). This is reflected in the developments and reforms of Nordic ECE curricula. While the curricula still reflect the social-pedagogical approach, they are also leaning more towards an Anglo-Saxon tradition of curricula design. However, policy-related steering is also often inherently inconsistent. For example, in the case of Sweden, it can be questioned how a linear, binding management system with pre-defined directions and with goals to strive towards in the policy documents, goes together with the prescribed pedagogical documentation based on non-linear, rhizome ideals (see Vallberg-Roth, 2013b). Furthermore, the translations of the regulations can also lead to results that contradict the objectives of the steering documents, for example in relation to how individually or activity oriented the documentation should be (cf. Alasuutari & Alasuutari, 2012).

The policy-related steering of assessment and documentation is often justified on scientific grounds, which leads us to the evidence-related dimension of ECE steering and guiding. This area is also linked with transnational actors and agencies (like the OECD) and international disciplinary discussions. Assessment and documentation tools are usually justified on the basis of particular theoretical approaches and/or standardization and evidence-based effectiveness, much like Second Step, a life skills programme developed in the USA. However, their sources of knowledge are commonly conflictive. Biesta (2007) takes a critical stance specifically on the notions of evidence-based or evidence-informed education – that is, on the idea that the scientific evidence generated by large-scale randomized and controlled studies should influence our educational decisions. He argues that they can lead to a focus on 'what works' instead of critically illuminating 'what is desirable' in education.

Biesta (2007) also discusses the third area that has an effect on the multi-documentation: the market-oriented dimension. This dimension has economic and commercial interests at its core, such as marketing-oriented profiles; management by objectives and results; and surveys measuring customer satisfaction in the spirit of New Public Management (NPM). According to Biesta, the current culture of liability that emphasizes the consumer's freedom of choice and the satisfaction of the buyer's needs as the principal goal of the market should not be confused with democracy. Consumers can choose from a fixed menu, but democracy exists only when citizens are initially involved in decisions about what is on the menu. We can relate this to studies about child documentation at the individual level that suggest that, even though children and parents seem to be involved in the formulation of individual development and educational plans (IDPs and IEPs), they cannot actually significantly influence the construction of these plans (Alasuutari & Karila, 2010; Alasuutari, 2010b; Vallberg-Roth, 2011a). Furthermore, we can also consider ECE institutions and the educators as consumers, since it is more and more common that assessment and documentation tools are designed for commercial markets, and that training in them is part of these commercial activities. Likewise, we have books (like this volume) that either market some specific documentation practice or discuss such practices more generally, which are, as a result, unavoidably commercial.

Finally, there is the civil-oriented dimension of steering and guiding. It refers to a sphere of seemingly voluntary actions around shared interests, experiences and values between fellows forming a network, which cannot be reduced to commercial, scientific or political interests (cf. Alexander, 2006; Dahlberg, Moss & Pence, 2007; Trondman, Lund & Mast, 2011). Parent associations exemplify this area as well as the Internet sites described in Chapter 8. On them, the parents discussed ECE documentation and also shared their doubts about the statements/opinions made by experts and scholars, and they expressed resistance to and criticisms of documentation and assessment. The Internet sites form a fairly new phenomenon in the civil sphere, and the ECE institutions do not perhaps recognize them as a source of feedback and as an assessment of themselves.

The four dimensions presented above constitute a steering and guiding system of ECE documentation that is not inherently consistent. Referring to Ferraris (2013), this whole can be described as a multitude and a system of inscriptions, registrations and documentations that make up the social reality and the institutional realities in it. The inscriptions, registrations and documentations are prior and contribute to the creation of a 'spirit' or spirits; this means, different meanings and collective intentionalities that are present in the social world. From a governance perspective (e.g. Rose, 1999b), the whole of the steering of ECE documentation can be understood as the junction of various discursive fields that imply different rationalities of government. The assessment and documentation carried out in ECE centres form the everyday meeting point of the four dimensions and the various discursive fields embedded in them. In the end, it is the teacher who translates and domesticates their influences in practice.

Teachers in multi-documentation

The contemporary Nordic curricula for ECE seem to place increased demands on teachers in relation to documentation (e.g. Lpfö98, 2010; Stakes, 2004). Besides the requirement to continually and systematically document and analyse the child's development and learning, teachers are also expected to involve the parents in the assessment and documentation and to communicate with them about different documentation practices (ibid.). In this book, we have proposed that the present-day ECE teachers can be described as multi-actors or trans-actors in the multi-documentation of ECE. This means that they (have to) move and switch between different forms, functions and mediums of assessment and documentation at micro, meso and macro levels, guiding their way through (or along) the both consistent and conflicting dimensions and discourses of the steering of ECE documentation.

In ECE institutions, documentation aims at specific functions. This means that documents are assumed to be 'strong' in a particular use (Ferraris, 2013). For example, in the Reggio Emilia tradition, the pedagogical documentation aims at empowering people – children, parents and educators – by challenging the dominant discourses and by opening up a critical and reflective practice (Dahlberg et al., 2007). In short, documentation aims at orienting the educator's gaze in specific ways and to particular directions.

Therefore, documentation also governs the professional, who uses it, and the objects of documentation, for instance, the child and/or the parent. It directs all the parties towards desirable characteristics and conduct in their (institutional) positions. In Foucault's (2007) terminology, documents are used as a technique of governance and power – both for the ends that can be valued as positive and for the ends that can be considered as negative. In this book, we have illuminated occasions in which the governance contradicted the functions that were defined for the documentation at the ideal level (for example, partnership) and, as a result, the documentation functioned in an opposite way. These findings also highlighted Ferraris' (2013) argument that a growth in the use of documentation has resulted in an increase of control, which is one of the effects of documentation within institutions.

However, the agency of ECE documentations is always intertwined with the agency of human actors. Although a document is framed by and constituted on specific notions and discourses, it is still the educator who deploys the material and who can change the frame and the use of it. Nevertheless, the ways in which these documents construct the social world is not often reflected upon (Ferraris, 2013). For example, Andersen-Østergaard, Hjort and Skytthe-Kaarsberg-Schmidt (2008) point out that documentation and evaluation are predominantly perceived as relatively positive and neutral activities that make learning visible without affecting it. Hence, they are not seen as tools that direct the teacher's gaze at an incident, which can then be constructed, for instance, as learning. ECE teachers may also view documentation and assessment as different phenomena, which are not intertwined (Vallberg-Roth, 2012b).

In practice, intensified ECE documentation requires an expanded symbolic competence from the teachers, including the skills to express, communicate and account for action. One challenge for them is to translate and transform everyday practices to a symbolic account (Andersen-Østergaard et al., 2008). The increased documentation highlights the importance of the possibilities of the teachers to develop their professional skills. They need skills to reflect on and scrutinize the frames and the knowledge sources of the documentation and assessment tools they are surrounded by. Furthermore, it is important that they are competent in taking a critical stance towards assessment and documentation. This critical stance could be characterized as interplay between believing and doubting games (cf. Elbow,

2008). 'The believing game is the disciplined practice of trying to be as welcoming or accepting as possible to every idea we encounter' (ibid., p. 1). However, in the doubting game the teacher 'can discover hidden contradictions, bad reasoning, or other weaknesses... especially, in the case of ideas that seem true or attractive' (ibid., p. 1). The doubting game can be used as a tool in order to scrutinize and test. The believing and doubting game may help the educators to choose among competing positions.

The increased use of documentation is also tied with professionalization as a means of quality assurance. For example, in a study by Simonsson and Markström (2013) the ECE teachers argued that parent–teacher discussions and the documentation they included could be interpreted as a relational teamwork. They considered the joint auditing of the child with the child's parent(s) as a support for themselves in their professionals work. Moreover, the teachers talked about the documentation and the conversations as a self-assessment practice. This meant that the talks and the documentation could be used to 'control oneself'; whether the teacher is 'following and living up to her/his professional assignment'. This could be understood as a way for teachers to control how they realize the curricula, but also as a tool to govern the professional subject (Foucault, 1991; Rose, O'Malley & Valverde, 2006).

However, professionally, child documentation is also a debated issue. Both in Sweden and Finland ECE teachers have, for example, complained in the media about the overload of 'paperwork' and the shortage of time to be with the children because of the paperwork. Indeed, we can question whether the increased documentation can make educators its prisoners and actually contradict their professional skills. Is it possible that the agency of documentation overcomes the agency of the educators and that documentalized practices start to follow the principle of 'papers first'? If quality is in documentation, do we still remember the importance of other professional skills, especially, interaction in producing quality?

Overall, there seems to be an idea that reality is possible to steer and control if we find the universal or the core in a complex situation in the world (Dahlberg, Moss & Pence, 1999), for instance, through observations, documentation and assessment. ECE documentation and the documentalized childhood can be interpreted as an expression of the growing tendencies of evaluation and assessment within the auditing society (Power, 1997). To find the best practice and evidence for decisions seem to be what the institutions and their actors strive to find. This means that teachers are also enticed to think that it is possible to measure everything, and that it is often something good that comes out of these practices.

In ECE, quality work refers commonly to the measurements and comparisons of different ECE systems at the transnational level and comparisons of different institutions at the national or local level. The term 'quality' is also frequently used in education policy, not only in relation to assurance, assessment, education, evaluation, accountability and control, but also as a means to create better conditions for children's lifelong learning (cf. Biesta, 2007; Dahlberg et al., 1999; Löfdahl & Pérez, 2009; Åsén & Vallberg-Roth, 2012). This focus on quality in education has been described as the *Quality Turn* (Segerholm, 2012), drawing attention to the need to critically scrutinize the language and policy of education quality, and, not least, the practices of measuring quality in education and its consequences. It is difficult to question the political intentions to improve education globally; what needs to be questioned is the Quality Turn, and its underlying assumptions about the meaning of education as a rational process with the primary goal of advancing economic growth. It is important to highlight the balance between the importance of standards, accountability and quality, and the parallel risks of standardization, over-regulation and control (Schwandt, 2012). In ECE, professional responsibilities may be described as moving from responsibility-through-confidence to responsibility-through-accountability. The critical question is how to balance accountability through measurements with human responsibility (cf. Schwandt, 2012; Segerholm, 2012), for example, with the responsibility for the children wanting to have 'a nice teacher' who is present in interaction. This is also a dilemma for the ECE teachers, as we have described in this book.

Note

1   For example, in Finland it is not rare that the parental forms enquire about the child's favourite toy (see Alasuutari & Karila, 2010). This query presumes that: first, toys are part of the child's daily life; second, she or he has some kind of ownership of the toys; and, third, she or he also has naturally different preferences regarding the toys.

APPENDIX

Notes on the data examples

The data examples include both written text and transcriptions of interviews and institutional interaction. The transcriptions have primarily follow the conventions of written language. However, they may show a few specific symbols:

/.../	A part of the text or talk has been erased, for example, because of the length of the example or repetitions in the talk.
(laughing)	Explanatory text is shown in parentheses to help the reader comprehend the context of the talk or text, or the concepts used in the example.
[	Start of overlapping talk in a transcription of face-to face interaction.

In the data extracts and in the text about them, each person has been identified according to the (institutional) position, for example, as the 'mother' or 'teacher'. This means that the identification of the parent also informs about the sex of the person. However, the labels 'mother' and 'father' do not imply that the person is always the biological parent. We use these labels only to denote the primary caretakers of the child and the main collaborators of early education, but we do not suggest anything more about their mutual relationship. When the name of a person – usually it is the child – is used in the data extract it is always a pseudonym. We have also identified the sex of the child when it has been denoted in the original talk or text. However, we have not shown the sex of the teachers in our examples. For example, our data set on parent-teacher talks includes recordings with both male and female teachers, although the latter are in the majority, as is the case in ECE generally. Because the teacher's sex has not been relevant in our examinations we have only used 'she' as a reference to the teacher.

REFERENCES

Åkerstrøm-Andersson, N. (2003). *Borgerens kontraktliggørelse* [The citizen contractualization]. Copenhagen: Hans Reitzels forlag.

Alanen, L. (2009). Generational order. In J. Qvortrup, W. A., Corsaro, & M.-S. Honig (Eds.), *The Palgrave Handbook of Childhood Studies* (pp. 159–74). Houndmills: Palgrave Macmillan.

Alasuutari, M. (2003). *Kuka lasta kasvattaa? Vanhemmuuden ja yhteiskunnallisen kasvatuksen suhde vanhempien puheessa* [Who is Raising the Child? Mothers and Fathers Constructing the Role of Parents and Professionals in Child Development]. Helsinki: Gaudeamus.

Alasuutari, M. (2009). What is so funny about children? Laughter in parent–practitioner interaction. *International Journal of Early Years Education, 17*(2), 105–18.

Alasuutari, M. (2010a). Striving at partnership: Parent–practitioner relationships in Finnish early educators' talk. *European Early Childhood Education Research Journal, 18*(2), 148–61.

Alasuutari, M. (2010b). *Suunniteltu lapsuus: Keskustelut lapsen varhaiskasvatuksesta päivähoidossa* [Planned Childhood: Parent–Practitioner Discussions on the Child's Education in Day Care]. Tampere: Vastapaino.

Alasuutari, M. (2013). Voicing the child? A case study in Finnish early childhood education. *Childhood*, published online before print, DOI: 10.1177/0907568213490205.

Alasuutari, M., & Karila, K. (2010). Framing the picture of the child. *Children & Society, 24*(2), 100–11.

Alasuutari, M., & Markström, A.-M. (2011). The making of the ordinary child in preschool. *Scandinavian Journal of Educational Research, 55*(5), 517–35.

Alasuutari, P. (1998). *An Invitation to Social Research*. London: Sage.

Alasuutari, P., & Alasuutari, M. (2012). The domestication of early childhood education plans in Finland. *Global Social Policy, 12*(2), 129–48.

Alasuutari, P., & Qadir, A. (forthcoming). Introduction: Interdependent national policy-making. In P. Alasuutari, & A. Qadir (Eds.), *National Policymaking: Domestication of Global Trends*. London: Routledge.

Alexander, J. C. (2006). *The Civil Sphere*. New York: Oxford University Press.

Andersen-Østergaard, P., Hjort, K., & Skytthe-Kaarsberg-Schmidt, L. (2008). *Dokumentation og evaluering mellem forvaltning og pædagogik* [Documentation and Evaluation of Management and Pedagogy]. Köpenhamn: Københavns Universitet.

132 References

Andréasson, I., & Asplund Carlsson, M. (2009). *Elevdokumentation:Textpraktiker i skolans värld* [Student Documentation:Text Practices in the World of Education]. Stockholm: Liber.

Åsén, G., & Vallberg-Roth, A.-C. (2012). *Utvärdering i förskolan – en översikt* [Evaluation in Preschool – An Overview]. Stockholm:Vetenskapsrådet.

Asp-Onsjö, L. (2010). *Dokumentation, föräldrainflytande och motstånd.* Konferensbidrag, 'Välfärdsstat i omvandling: Reglerad barndom och oregerlig ungdom?' [Seminar paper. Documentation, Parent's Influence and Resistance]. 2010-10-28/29, Malmö högskola.

Atkinson, P., & Coffey, A. (2011). Analysing documentary realities. In D. Silverman (Ed.), *Qualitative Research 3rd Edition* (pp. 77–92). London: Sage.

Baker, C., & Keogh, J. (1995). Accounting for achievement in parent-teacher interviews. *Human Studies, 18*(2–3), 263–300.

Ball, S. (2006). *Education Policy and Social Class:The Selected Works of Stephen J. Ball.* London: Routledge.

Barad, K. (2003). Posthumanist performativity: Toward an understanding of how matter comes to matter. *Signs: Journal of Women in Culture and Society, 28*(3), 801–31.

Barad, K. (2007). *Meeting the Universe Halfway: Quantum Physics and the Entanglement of Matter and Meaning.* Durham, NC: Duke University Press.

Bartholdsson, Å. (2007). *Med facit i hand: Normalitet, elevskap och vänlig maktutövning i två svenska skolor* [Constructing the Pupil: Normality and Benevolent Government]. Diss. Stockholm universitet: Antropologiska institutionen.

Bauman, Z. (2007). *Consuming Life.* Cambridge: Polity.

Beck, U. (1992). *Risk Society – Towards a New Modernity.* London: Sage.

Bennet, R. E. (2011). Formative assessment a critical review: Assessment in education. *Principles, Policy & Practice, 18*(1), 5–25.

Bennett, J. (2010). Pedagogy in early childhood services with special reference to Nordic approaches. *Psychological Science and Education, 3,* 16–21.

Berg, M. (2010). *Många rader om en begreppsapparat* [Many lines about a conceptual framework]. Retrieved May 20, 2011 from http://www.martinberg.se/2010/02/10/manga-rader-om-en-begreppsapparat/#more-250.

Biesta, G. (2007). Why 'what works' won't work: Evidence-based practice and the democratic deficit of educational research. *Educational theory, 57*(1), 1–22.

Biesta, G. (2009). *Good education:What it is and why we need it.* Inaugural Lecture.The Stirling Institute of Education.

Biesta, G. (2011). *God utbildning i mätningens tidevarv* [Good Education in an Era of Measurement]. Stockholm: Liber.

Bjervås, L.-L. (2011). *Samtal om barn och pedagogisk dokumentation som bedömningspraktik i förskolan. En diskursanalys* [Teachers' views of preschool children in relation to pedagogical documentation – A discourse analysis]. *Gothenburg Studies in Educational Sciences 312.* Gothenborg: Acta Universitatis Gothoburgensis. Retrieved 17 September 2013 from https://gupea.ub.gu.se/bitstream/2077/25731/1/gupea_2077_25731_1.pdf.

Black, P., & Wiliam, D. (1998). *Inside the Black Box: Raising Standards Through Classroom Assessment.* London: King's College London, School of Education.

Black, P., & Wiliam, D. (2009). Developing the theory of formative assessment. *Educational Assessment Evaluation and Accountability, 21*(1), 5–31.

Bloch, M. N., Holmlund, K., Moqvist, I., & Popkewitz, T. S. (2003). *Governing Children, Families and Education: Restructuring the Welfare State.* New York: Palgrave Macmillan.

Borg, C., & Mayo, P. (2001). From 'adjuncts' to 'subjects': Parental involvement in a working class community. *British Journal of Sociology of Education, 22*(2), 245–66.

Brin, D. (2006). *The Transparent Society: Will Technology Force us to Choose Between Privacy and Freedom?* New York: Perseus Books.

Bronfenbrenner, U. (1979). *The Ecology of Human Development: Experiments by Nature and Design.* Cambridge, MA: Harvard University Press.

Bronfenbrenner, U., & Morris, P. A. (2006). The bioecological model of human development. *Handbook of child psychology (6th ed.). Vol 1, Theoretical models of human development* (pp. 793–828). Hoboken, NJ: John Wiley & Sons.

Bruhn Jensen, K. (2011). New media old methods: Internet methodologies and the online/offline divide. In M. Consalvo, & C. Ess (Eds.), *The Handbook of Internet Studies* (pp. 43–58). Oxford: Blackwell.

Buchanan, D., & Dawson, P. (2007). Discourse and audience: Organizational change as multi-story process. *Journal of Management Studies, 44*(5), 669–86.

Bugge, N. (2010). Erfaringer med TRAS i barnehagen [Experiences of TRAS in ECE]. *Nordic Early Childhood Education Research, 3*(3), 209–17.

Buldu, M. (2010). Making learning visible in kindergarten classrooms: Pedagogical documentation as a formative assessment technique. *Teacher and Teacher Education, 26*(7), 1439–49.

Bundgaard, H., & Gullov, E. (2008). Targeting immigrant children: Disciplinary rationales in Danish preschools. In N. Dyck (Ed.), *Exploring Regimes of Discipline: The Dynamics of Restraint* (pp. 42–56). New York: Bergham Books.

Burr, V. (2003). *Social Constructionism.* London: Routledge.

Canella, G. S. (1997). *Deconstructing Early Childhood Education: Social Justice & Revolution. Rethinking Childhood 2.* New York: Peter Lang.

Carr, M., & Lee, W. (2012). *Learning Stories: Constructing Learner Identities in Early Education.* London: Sage.

Castelli, S., & Pepe, A. (2008). School–parents relationships: A bibliometric study on 40 years of scientific publications. *International Journal about Parents in Education, 2*(1), 1–12.

Clark, A. (2005). Ways of seeing: Using the Mosaic approach to listen to young children's perspectives. In A. Clark, A. T. Kjørholt, & P. Moss (Eds.), *Beyond Listening: Children's Perspectives on Early Childhood Services* (pp. 29–49). Bristol: The Policy Press.

Colliander, M.-A., Stråhle, L., & Wehner-Godée, C. (Eds.) (2010). *Om värden och omvärlden: Pedagogik praktik och teori med inspiration från Reggio Emilia* [About Values and the World: Teaching Practice and Theory, Inspired by Reggio Emilia]. Stockholm: Stockholms universitets förlag.

Cooren, F. (2004). Textual agency: How texts do things in organizational settings. *Organization, 11*(3), 373–93. DOI: 10.1177/1350508404041998.

Corsaro, W. (1997). *The Sociology of Childhood.* Thousand Oaks, CA: Pine Forge Press.

Crozier, G., & Davies, J. (2007) Hard to reach parents or hard to reach schools? A discussion of home–school relations, with particular reference to Bangladeshi and Pakistani parents. *British Educational Research Journal, 33*(3), 295–313.

Crozier, G., Reay, D., James, D., Jamieson, F., Hollingworth, S., Williams, K., & Beedell, P. (2008). White middle class parents, identities, educational choice and the urban comprehensive school: Dilemmas, ambivalence and moral ambiguity. *British Journal of Sociology of Education, 29*(3), 261–72.

Dahlberg, G., & Lenz-Taguchi, H. (1995). *Förskola och skola: Om två skilda traditioner och om visionen om en mötesplats* [Preschool and School; Two Different Traditions and a Vision of a Meeting Place]. Stockholm: HLS.

Dahlberg, G., Moss, P., & Pence, A. (1999). *Beyond Quality in Early Childhood Education and Care: Postmodern Perspectives.* London: Routledge.

Dahlberg, G., Moss, P., & Pence, A. R. (2007). *Beyond Quality in Early Childhood Education and Care. Languages of Evaluation* (2nd ed.). London: Routledge.

Daun, H. (1997). Omstrukturering av det svenska skolsystemet: Gensvar på globaliserings-tendenser eller nationella krav [Restructuration of the Swedish school system: Response to tendencies of globalization or national demands?]. *Pedagogisk forskning i Sverige, 2*(3), 161–81.

Davies, B. (1993). *Shards of Glass: Children Reading and Writing Beyond Gendered Identities.* Cresskill, NJ: Hampton Press.

Davies, B., & Banks, C. (1995). The gender trap. In J. Holland, & M. Blair (Eds.), *Debates and Issues in Feminist Research and Pedagogy: A Reader.* London: The Open University.

Davies, B., & Harré, R. (1990). Positioning: The discursive production of selves. *Journal of Theory and Social Behaviour, 20*(1), 43–63.

de Carvallho, M. E. P. (2001). *Rethinking Family–School Relations: A Critique of Parental Involvement in Schooling.* London: Lawrence Erlbaum Associates.

Dean, M. (1999). *Governmentality: Power and Rule in Modern Society.* London: Sage.

Deleuze, G., & Guattari, F. (1987). *A Thousand Plateaus.* Minneapolis: University of Minnesota Press.

Donzelot, J. (1997). *The Policing of Families.* Baltimore, MD: Johns Hopkins University Press.

Drasgow, E., Yell, M. L., & Robinson, Rowand (2001). Developing legally correct and educationally appropriate IEPs. *Remedial and Special Education, 22*(6), 359–73.

Drew, P., and Heritage, J. (1992). Analyzing talk at work: An introdution. In P. Drew and J. Heritage (Eds.), *Talk at Work: Interaction in Institutional Settings* (pp. 3–65). Cambridge: Cambridge University Press.

Driscoll, V., & Rudge, C. (2005). Channels for listening to young children and parents. In A. Clark, A. T. Kjørholt, & P. Moss (Eds.), *Beyond Listening: Children's Perspectives on Early Childhood Services* (pp. 91–110). Bristol: The Policy Press.

Ds 2009:25. Den nya skollagen – för kunskap, valfrihet och trygghet [The new Education Act – for knowledge, free choice and safety].

Duits, L. (2008). *Multi-Girl-Culture: An Ethnography of Doing Identity.* Amsterdam: University Press.

Elbow, P. (2008). *The Believing Game – Methodological Believing.* Retrieved June 20, 2013 from http://works.bepress.com/peter_elbow/20.

Elfström, I. (2004). *Varför individuella utvecklingsplaner? – en studie om ett nytt utvärderingsverktyg i förskolan* [Why Individual Development Plans?: A Study of a New Evaluation Tool in Preschool]. Stockholm: Lärarhögskolan i Stockholm.

Englund, T. (2010). Questioning the parental right to educational authority: Arguments for a pluralistic public education system. *Education Inquiry, 1*(3), 235–58.

Epstein, J. L. (1995). School/family/community partnerships: Caring for the children we share. *Phi Delta Kappa, 76*(9), 701–12.

Espenakk, U. (2003). *TRAS Schema för registrering av språkutveckling hos barn* [TRAS scheme for registering children's language development]. DK, Herning: www.SPF-Utbildning.com.

Etscheidt, S. (2006). Behavioral intervention plans: Pedagogical and legal analysis of issues. *Behavioral Disorders, 31*(2), 223–43.

European Communities (2007). *Key Competences for Lifelong Learning: European Reference Framework.* Retrieved 8 March 2013 from http://ec.europa.eu/dgs/education_culture/publ/pdf/ll-learning/keycomp_en.pdf.

Fejes, A., & Dahlstedt, M. (2012). *The Confessing Society: Foucault, Confession and Practices of Lifelong Learning.* London: Routledge.

Ferraris, M. (2013). *Documentality: Why It is Necessary to Leave Traces* (R. Davies, Trans.). New York: Fordham University Press.

File, N. (2001). Family–Professional Partnerships: Practice That Matches Philosophy. *Young Children, 56*(4), 70–4.

Foot, H., Howe, C., Cheyne, B., Terras, M., & Rattray, C. (2002). Parental Participation and Partnership in Pre-School Provision. *International Journal of Early Years Education, 10*(1), 5–19.

Forsberg, L. (2007). Involving parents through school letters: Mothers, fathers and teachers negotiating children's education and rearing. *Ethnography & Education, 2*(3), 273–88.

Forsberg, L. (2009). *Involved Parenthood: Everyday Lives of Swedish Middle-Class Families.* Linköping Studies in Arts and Science No. 473. Linköping: Linköping University, Department of Child Studies.

Foucault, M. (1991). Governmentality. In G. Burchell, C. Gordon, & P. Miller (Eds.), *The Foucault Effect: Studies in Governmentality. With Two Lectures by and an Interview With Michael Foucault* (pp. 87–104). Chicago: University of Chicago Press.

Foucault, M. (1994). *The Order of Things.* London and New York: Tavistock/Routledge.

Foucault, M. (2003). On the genealogy of ethics: An overview of work in progress. In P. Rainbow, & N. Rose (Eds.), *The Essential Foucault: Selections From the Essential Works of Foucault 1954–1984.* New York: The New Press.

Foucault, M. (2007). *Security, Territory, Population: Lectures at the College de France, 1977–78.* Basingstoke: Palgrave Macmillan.

Foucault, M. (2008). *Diskursernas kamp: Texter i urval av Thomas Götselius och Ulf Olsson* [The Struggle of the Discourses. A Selection of Texts by Thomas Götselius and Ulf Olsson]. Stockholm: Brutus Östlings Bokförlag Symposion.

Franklin, B. M., Bloch, M. N., & Popkewitz, T. S. (2003). *Educational Partnerships and the State: The Paradoxes of Governing Schools, Children, and Families.* New York: Palgrave Macmillan.

Garfinkel, H. (1984). *Studies in Ethnomethodology.* Cambridge: Polity.

Gergen, K. J. (1999). *An Invitation to Social Construction.* London: Sage.

Gergen, K. J. (2009). *Relational Being: Beyond Self and Community.* Oxford: Oxford University Press.

Giddens, A. (1997). *Modernity and Self-Identity: Self and Society in the Late Modern World.* Oxford: Polity Press in association with Blackwell.

Giedd, J. (2007). *Hjärnan fullvuxen först vid 25!* [The brain fully grown first at 25!] Retrieved 16 November 2010 from http://www.uidfuturemap.se/page25/page5/page5.html.

Giota, J. (2006). Självbedöma, bedöma eller döma?: Om elevers motivation, kompetens och prestationer i skolan [Self-evaluation, evaluation or judgement? About pupils' motivation, competence and achievement in school]. *Pedagogisk forskning i Sverige, 11*(2), 94–115.

Gitz-Johansen, T. (2004). The incompetent child: Representations of ethnic minority children. In H. Brembeck, B. Johansson, & J. Kampmann (Eds.), *Beyond the Competent Child: Exploring Contemporary Childhoods in the Nordic Welfare Societies* (pp. 199–225). Roskilde: Roskilde University Press.

Gjems, L. (2010). Kartlegging av barns språk: Godt for hvem – godt for hva? [Screening of children's language: Who is it good for? What is it good for?]. *Nordic Early Childhood Education Research, 3*(3), 175–82.

Goffman, E. (1961). *Asylums: Essays on the Social Situation of Mental Patients and other Inmates.* Middlesex: Penguin Books.

Goffman, E. (1967). *Interaction Ritual. Essays on Face-to-face Behavior.* Chicago: Aldine.

Granbom, I. (2011). *Vi har nästan blivit för bra: Lärares sociala representationer av förskolan som pedagogisk praktik* [We have Become Almost too Good: Teachers' Social Representations of Pre-School as a Pedagogical Practice]. Diss. School of Education and Communication. Jönköping: Jönköping University.

Grimen, H. (2009). Debatten om evidensbasering – noen utfordringer [The debate about evidence-based approach – some challenges]. In H. Grimen, & L. I. Terum (Eds.), *Evidensbasert profesjonsutøvelse* [Evidence-based professional practice] (pp. 191–222). Oslo: Abstrakt forlag AS.

Gubrium, J. F., & Holstein, J. A. (1997). *The New Language of Qualitative Method.* New York: Oxford University Press.

Gundem, B. B. (1997). Läroplansarbete som didaktisk verksamhet [Curriculum work as a didaktik activity]. In M. Uljens (Ed.), *Didaktik – teori, reflektion och praktik* [Didaktik – Theory, Reflection and Practice] (pp. 246–67). Lund: Studentlitteratur.

Gundem, B. B., & Hopmann, S. (Eds.) (1998). *Didaktik and/or Curriculum: An international Dialogue.* New York: Peter Lang.

Gustafsson, J. (2004). Portföljer, en bärande idé? [Portfolios, a fundamental idea?] *Studies in Educational Policy and Educational Philosophy* 2004:2. Retrieved 17 February 2010 from http://www.upi.artisan.se/docs/Doc230.pdf.

Gustavsson, L. H. (2010). Radio conversation with the doctor: L.H. Gustavsson on the perfect parent. Retrieved April, 26 2010 from http://sverigesradio.se/sida/artikel.aspx?prog ramid=3381&artikel=2728785.

Haakana, M. (2001). Laughter as a patient's resource: Dealing with delicate aspects of medical interaction. *Text, 21*(1/2), 187–219.

Hallgarten, J. (2000). *Parents Exist, OK!? Issues and Visions for Parent–School Relationships.* London: Ippr.

Hanafin, J., & Lynch, A. (2002). Peripheral voices: Parental involvement, social class, and education disvantages. *British Journal of Sociology in Education, 23*(1), 35–49.

Harrison, C., & Howard, S. (2009). *Inside the Primary Black Box: Assessment for Learning and Early Years Classrooms.* London: GL Assessment, Kings College.

Harvey, D. (2005). *A Brief History of Neoliberalism.* Oxford: Oxford University Press.

Hasenfeld, Y., Rafferty, J. A., & Zald, M. N. (1987). The welfare state, citizenship, and bureaucratic encounters. *Annual Review of Sociology, 13,* 387–415.

Hendrick, H. (2004). *Child Welfare and Social Policy: An Essential Reader.* Bristol: Policy.

Hepburn, A., & Potter, J. (2004). Discourse analytic practice. In C. Seale, G. Gobo, J. F. Gubrium, & D. Silverman (Eds.), *Qualitative Research Practice* (pp. 180–96). London: Sage.

Hjort, K. (2008). *Hvorfor taler vi om kompetenceindikatorer? Er kompetenceindikatorer et kvalificerende styringsredskab? En analyse af et styringsredskab og dets konsekvenser for det pædagogiske arbejde* [Why are We Talking About Competence Indicators? Are Competence Indicators a Qualifying Steering Tool? An Analysis of a Steering Tool and Its Impact on the Educational Work]. Köpenhamn: BUPL. Retrieved 22 February 2013 from http://www.bupl.dk/iwfile/AGMD-7VQJWH/$file/kompetenceindikatorer_ web.pdf.

Holstein, J. A., & Gubrium, J. F. (2007). *Handbook of Constructionist Research.* New York: The Guilford Press.

Hosp, J. L., & Reschly, D. J. (2004). Disproportionate representation of minority students in special education: Academic, demographic, and economic predictors. *Exceptional Children, 70*(2), 185–99.

Hughes, P., & MacNaughton, G. (2000). Consensus, dissensus or community: The politics of parent involvement in early childhood education. *Contemporary Issues in Early Childhood, 1*(3), 241–58.

Hultqvist, K. (1990) *Förskolebarnet: En konstruktion för gemenskapen och den individuella frigörelsen* [The Preschool Child: A Construction for the Community and for the Individual Liberation]. Diss. Stockholm: Stehag, Symposion.

Hundeide, K. (2006). *Sociokulturella ramar för barns utveckling: Barns livsvärldar* [Sociocultural Frames for Children's Development: Children's Life Worlds]. Lund: Studentlitteratur.

James, A. (2007). Giving voice to children's voices: Practices and problems, pitfalls and potentials. *American Anthropologist, 109*(2), 261–72.

James, A. (2012). 'Child-centredness' and 'the child': The cultural politics of nursery schooling in England. In A. T. Kjørholt, & J. Qvortrup (Eds.), *The Modern Child and the Flexible Labour Market: Early Childhood Education and Care* (pp. 111–27). Hampshire: Palgrave Macmillan.

James, A., & James, A. (2008). Changing childhood in the UK: Reconstructing discourses of 'risk' and 'protection'. In A. James, & A. James (Eds.), *Changing Childhood in the UK: Reconstructing Discourses of 'Risk' and 'Protection'* (pp. 105–27). Basingstoke: Palgrave Macmillan.

James, A., Jenks, C., & Prout, A. (1998). *Theorizing Childhood*. Cambridge: Polity Press.

James, A., & Prout, A. (1997). *Constructing and Reconstructing Childhood: Contemporary Issues in the Sociological Study of Childhood*. London: Falmer Press.

Jensen, A., Broström, S., & Hansen, O. H. (2010). Critical perspectives on Danish early childhood education and care: Between the technical and the political. *Early Years – An International Journal of Research and Development, 30*(3), 243–54.

Jepperson, R. L. (1991). Institutions, institutional effects, and institutionalism. In W. W. Powell, & P. J. DiMaggio (Eds.), *The New Institutionalism in Organizational Analysis* (pp. 143–63). Chicago: The University of Chicago Press.

Johansen-Lyngseth, E. (2010). Forebyggende muligheter ved dynamisk språkkartlegging med TRAS-observasjoner i barnehagen [Preventive opportunities for dynamic language mapping with TRAS observations in ECE]. *Nordic Early Childhood Education Research, 3*(3), 219–25.

Juhila, K. (2003). Creating a 'bad' client: Disalignment of institutional identities in social work interaction. In C. Hall, K. Juhila, N. Parton, & T. Pösö (Eds.), *Constructing Clienthood in Social Work and Human Services: Interaction, Identities and Practices* (pp. 83–95). London: Jessica Kingsley.

Jungkvist, E., & Sandell, M. (2002). *Ämnes- och visningsportfolio: Idémallar för grundskolans senare år* [Subject and Showing Portfolio: Idea Templates for Secondary School]. Stockholm: Förlagshuset GOTHIA.

Kampmann, J. (2004). Societaliztion of childhood: New opportunities? New demands? In H. Brembeck, B. Johansson, & J. Kampmann (Eds.), *Beyond the Competent Child: Exploring Contemporary Childhoods in the Nordic Welfare Societies* (pp. 127 52). Roskilde: Roskilde University Press.

Kampmann, J. (2005). Restaurative tendenser i uddannelsespolitikken – når livet bliver til test og kanon. *Dansk pædagogisk tidskrift, 4*, 75–9.

Karila, K. (2006). The significance of parent–practitioner interaction in early childhood education. *Zeitschrift für Qualitative Bildungs-, Betratungs- und Sozialforschung* (Heft 1), 7–24.

Karila, K. (2012). A Nordic perspective on early childhood education and care policy. *European Journal of Education, 47*(4), 584–95.

Karila, K., & Alasuutari, M. (2012). Drawing partnership on paper: How do the forms for individual educational plans prescribe parent–teacher relationship? *International Journal about Parents in Education, 6*(1), 15–27.

Karlsen Baek, U.-D. (2010). 'We are the professionals': A study of teachers' views on parental involvement in school. *British Journal of Sociology of Education, 31*(3), 323–35.

Keyes, C. R. (2002). A way of thinking about parent/teacher partnerships for teachers. *International Journal of Early Years Education, 10*(3), 177–91.

Kimber, B. (2011). *Primary Prevention of Mental Health Problems Among Children and Adolescents Through Social and Emotional Training in School.* Stockholm: Karolinska institutet.

Kimber, B., & Petré, C. (2009). *SET i förskolan: Handbok i konsten att praktisera social och emotionell träning* [SET in Preschool: Guide in the Art of Practicing Social and Emotional Training]. Malmö: Gleerup.

Kjørholt, A. T. (2005). The competent child and 'the right to be oneself': Reflections on children as fellow citizens in an early childhood centre. In A. Clark, A. T. Kjørholt, & P. Moss (Eds.), *Beyond Listening: Children's Perspectives on Early Childhood Services* (pp. 151–73). Bristol: The Policy Press.

Kress, G. (2003). *Literacy in the New Media Age.* London: Routledge.

Kristjansson, B. (2006). The making of Nordic childhoods. In J. Einarsdottir, & J. T. Wagner (Eds.), *Nordic Childhoods and Early Education: Philosophy, Research, Policy, and Practice in Denmark, Finland, Iceland, Norway and Sweden* (pp. 13–42). Greenwich, CT: Information Age Publishing.

Kristoffersson, M. (2008). *Lokala styrelser med föräldramajoritet i grundskolan* [Local Boards With a Majority of Parents in Primary School]. Diss. Umeå: Umeå universitet, Samhällsvetenskaplig fakultet.

Kumpfer, K. L., & Alvarado, R. (2003). Family-strengthening approaches for the prevention of youth problem behaviors. *American Psychologist, 58*(6/7), 457–65.

Lahaye, W., Nimal, P., & Couvreur, P. (2001). Young people's representations of school and family relationships in Belgium. In S. Smit, K. van der Wolf, & P. Slegers. *In a Bridge to the Future* (pp. 201–12). Nijmegen: ITS.

Lappalainen, S. (2004). They say it's a cultural matter: Gender and ethnicity at preschool. *European Educational Research Journal, 3*(3), 642–56.

Lareau, A. (2000). *Home Advantage: Social Class and Parental Intervention in Elementary Education.* New York: Rowman & Littlefield.

Latour, B. (1994). Pragmatogonies: A mythical account of how humans and nonhumans swap properties. *American Behavioral Scientist, 37*(6), 791–808.

Latour, B. (1996). On interobjectivity. *Mind, Culture, and Activity, 3*(4), 228–45.

Latour, B. (2005). *Reassembling the Social: An Introduction to Actor-Network-Theory.* New York: Oxford University Press.

Lenz-Taguchi, H. (2000). *Emancipation och motstånd: Dokumentation och kooperativa läroprocesser i förskolan* [Emancipation and Resistance: Documentation Practices and Co-Operative Learning-Processes in Early Childhood Education]. Diss. Stockholm: Lärarhögskolan i Stockholm.

Lenz-Taguchi, H. (2010). *Going Beyond the Theory/Practice Divide in Early Childhood Education: Introducing an Intra-Active Pedagogy.* London: Routledge.

Lenz-Taguchi, H. (2012). *Pedagogisk dokumentation som aktiv agent: Introduktion till intra-aktiv pedagogik* [Pedagogic Documentation as an Active Agent: An Introduction to an Intra-active Pedagogy]. Malmö: Gleerup.

Lidholt, B. (2001). *EDUcare eller EduCARE – Förskolepersonalens dilemma: Omsorgsbegreppet i förskolan* [EDUcare or EduCARE – The preschool teacher's dilemma: The concept of care in preschool]. *Working Papers on Childhood and the Study of Children* (pp. 62–70). Linköping: Department of Child Studies/Tema Barn, University of Linköping.

Lindberg, V. (2005). Svensk forskning om bedömning och betyg 1990–2005. [Swedish research on assessment and scores 1990-2005]. *Studies in Educational Policy and Educational Philosophy, E-journal,* 2005:1. Retrieved 20 May 2013 from http://forskning.edu.uu.se/upi/SITE_Docs/Doc233.pdf.

Lindberg, V. (2011). Betyg och bedömning i svensk didaktisk forskning [Grades and assessment in Swedish educational research]. In L. Lindström, V. Lindberg, & A. Pettersson

(Eds.) (2:a uppl.), *Pedagogisk bedömning: Om att dokumentera, bedöma och utveckla kunskap* [Educational Assessment: About Documenting, Assessing and Developing Knowledge] (pp. 235–67). Stockholm: Stockholms universitets förlag.

Lindensjö, B., & Lundgren, U. P. (2000). *Utbildningsreformer och politisk styrning* [Educational Reforms and Political Governance]. Stockholm: HLS Förlag.

Lindgren, A., & Sparrman, A. (2003). Om att bli dokumenterad: Etiska aspekter på förskolans arbete med dokumentation [Getting documented: Ethical aspect of documentation in preschool]. *Pedagogisk Forskning i Sverige, 8*(1), 58–69.

Lindström, L. (2011). Portföljmetodik i estetiska ämnen [Portfolio method in the arts]. In L. Lindström, V. Lindberg, & A. Pettersson (Eds.) (2:a uppl.), *Pedagogisk bedömning: Om att dokumentera bedöma och utveckla kunskap* [Educational Assessment: About Documenting, Assessing and Developing Knowledge] (pp. 155–88). Stockholm: Stockholms universitets förlag.

Lindström, L., Lindberg, V., & Pettersson, A. (Eds.) (2011). *Pedagogisk bedömning: Om att dokumentera bedöma och utveckla kunskap* [Educational Assessment: About Documenting, Assessing and Developing Knowledge] (2nd ed.). Stockholm: Stockholms universitets förlag.

Linell, P., & Bredmar, M. (1996). Reconstructing topical sensitivity: Aspects of face-work in talks between midwives and expectant mothers. *Research on Language and Social Interaction, 29*(4), 347–79.

Löfdahl, A., & Pérez, P. H. (2010). Den synliggjorda förskolan [The visualized preschool]. In C. Lundahl, & M. Folke Fichtelius (Eds.) *Bedömning i och av skolan – praktik, principer, politik* [Assessment in and of School – Practice, Principles, Policies] (pp. 71–84). Lund: Studentlitteratur.

Löwenborg, L., & Gislason, B. (2010a). *StegVis 1 socialt och emotionellt lärande för barn i åldrarna 4–6 år* [Second Step 1 Social and Emotional Learning for Children Aged 4–6 Years]. Herning, DK, Specialpedagogiskt förlag. Retrieved 7 September 2012 from http:// www.gislasonlowenborg.com/StegVis.html#Ursprung.

Löwenborg, L., & Gislason, B. (2010b). *START: Livskunskap för de minsta* [START: Life Knowledge for the Youngest]. DK, Herning: SPF-utbildning.com.

Lpfö98. (2010). *Läroplan för förskolan reviderad 2010* [Curriculum for the Preschool]. Stockholm: Ministry of Education and Science.

Lutz, K. (2009). *Kategoriseringar av barn i förskoleåldern: Styrning & administrativa processer* [Categorization of Preschool Children: Governance and Administrative Processes]. Malmö: Lärarutbildningen, Malmö Studies in Educational Sciences, 2009: 44.

Määttä, M., & Kalliomaa-Puha, L. (2005). Sopivaksi kasvattava yhteiskunta? Koti, koulu ja uusi sopimuksellisuus [Appropriating society? Home, school and the new contractualism]. In K. Rantala, & P. Sulkunen (Eds.), *Projektiyhteiskunnan kääntöpuolia* [The Project Society Inside Out] (pp. 179–93). Helsinki: Gaudeamus.

MacNaughton, G. (2000). *Rethinking Gender in Early Childhood Educations.* London: Paul Chapman.

Mäkitalo, Å. (2005). The record as a formative tool: A study of immanent pedagogy in the practice of vocational guidance. *Qualitative Social Work, 4*(4), 431–49.

Markström, A.-M. (2005). *Förskolan som normaliseringspraktik: En etnografisk studie* [Preschool as a Normalizing Practice: An Ethnographic Study]. Linköping: Pedagogic Practices, University of Linköping.

Markström, A.-M. (2006). Utvecklingssamtalet – ett möte mellan hem och institution [The developmental talk – an encounter between the home and the institution]. *Skapande Vetande.* Linköping: University of Linköping.

Markström, A.-M. (2008). Förskolans utvecklingssamtal: Ett komplex av aktiviteter i tid och rum [The parent–teacher conference: A complex of activities in time and space]. *Educare, 1*, 51–67.

Markström, A.-M. (2009). The parent–teacher conference in the Swedish preschool: A study of an ongoing process as a 'pocket of local order'. *Contemporary Issues in Early Childhood*, *10*(2), 122–32.

Markström, A.-M. (2010). Talking about children's strategies to show resistance in preschool. *Journal of Early Childhood Research*, *8*(3), 303–14.

Markström, A.-M. (2011a). To involve parents in the assessment of the child in developmental talks. *Early Childhood Education Journal*, *38*(6), 465–74.

Markström, A.-M. (2011b). 'Soft governance' i förskolans utvecklingssamtal ['Soft governance' in developmental talks in preschool]. *Educare*, *2*, 57–75.

Markström, A.-M., & Halldén, G. (2009) Children's strategies for agency in preschool. *Children and Society*, *23*(2), 112–22.

Markström, A.-M., & Simonsson, M. (2011). Constructions of girls in preschool parent–teacher conference. *International Journal of Early Childhood*, *43*(1), 23–41.

Markström, A.-M., & Simonsson, M. (2013). *Utvecklingssamtal: Kommunikation mellan hem och förskola* [Developmental Talk: Communication Between Home and Preschool]. Lund: Studentlitteratur.

Mayall, B. (2002). *Towards a Sociology of Childhood: Thinking from Children's Lives*. Buckingham: Open University Press.

Maybin, J., Woodhead, M., Moss, P., Dillon, J., & Statham, J. (2000). The 'child in need' and 'the rich child': Discourses, constructions and practice. *Critical Social Policy, 20*(2), 233–54.

Mazeland, H., & Berenst, J. (2008). Sorting pupils in a report-card meeting: Categorization in a situated activity system. *Text and Talk*, *28*(1), 55–78.

Mezirow, J., Marsick, V. J., Hart, M. U., Heany, T. W., Horton, A. I., Kennedy, W. B., Roth, I., Gould, R.C., Kitchener, K. S., King, P. M., Brookfield, S., Dominicé, P. F., Lukinsky, J., Green, M., Candy, P.C., Deshler, D., & Peters, J. (1990). *Fostering Critical Reflection in Adulthood: A Guide to Transformative an Emancipatory Learning*. San Francisco, CA: Jossey-Bass.

Miller, P., & Rose, N. (2008). *Governing the Present: Administering Economic, Social and Personal Life*. Oxford: Polity.

Mishler, E. (1984). *The Discourse of Medicine: Dialectis of Medical Interviews*. New Jersey: Ablex.

Nichols, S., & Jurvansuu, S. (2008). Partnership in integrated early childhood services: An analysis of policy framings in education and human services. *Contemporary Issues in Early Childhood, 9*(2), 118–30.

Niikko, A. (2006). Finnish daycare: Caring, education, and instruction. In J. Einarsdottir, & J. T. Wagner (Eds.), *Nordic Childhoods and Early Education: Philosophy, Research, Policy, and Practice in Denmark, Finland, Iceland, Norway, and Sweden* (pp. 133–58). Greenwich, CT: Information Age Publishing.

Nordin-Hultman, E. (2004). *Pedagogiska miljöer och barns subjektsskapande* [The Pedagogical Environment and Children's Constructions of Subjectivity]. Stockholm: Liber.

OECD. (2001). *Starting Strong: Early Childhood Education and Care*. Paris: Organization for Economic Cooperation and Development.

OECD. (2006). *Starting Strong II*. Paris: Organisation for Economic Cooperation and Development.

OECD. (2012). *Starting Strong III: A Quality Toolbox for Early Childhood Education and Care*. OECD Publishing. Retrieved 20 May 2013 from http:dx.doi.org/10.1787/9789264123564-en.

Østrem, S. (2010). Verdibasert formål eller vilkårlige detaljmål? [Value based objectives, or random, specific goals?] *Nordic Early Childhood Education Research, 3*(3), 191–203.

Palla, L. (2011). *Med blicken på barnet: Om olikheter inom förskolan som diskursiv praktik* [With a Gaze on the Child: About Differences in Preschool as Discursive Practices]. Malmö: Malmö högskola.

Parton, N. (2006). *Safeguarding Childhood: Early Intervention, and Surveillance in a Late Modern Society*. Basingstoke: Palgrave Macmillan.

Parton, N. (2010). 'From dangerousness to risk': The growing importance of screening and surveillance systems for safeguarding and promoting the well-being of children in England. *Health, Risk & Society, 12*(1), 51–64.

Parton, N. (2011). Child protection and safeguarding in England: Changing and competing conceptions of risk and their implications for social work. *British Journal of Social Work, 41*(5), 854–75.

Peräkylä, A. (1995). *AIDS Counselling: Institutional Interaction and Clinical Practice*. Cambridge: Cambridge University Press.

Persson, S., & Tallberg Broman, I. (2002). 'Det är ju ett annat jobb' – Förskollärare, grundskollärare och lärarstuderande om professionell identitet i konflikt och förändring ['That's a quite different job' – The delimitations of the teacher profession and the teacher's social education responsibility]. *Pedagogisk Forskning i Sverige, 7*(4), 257–278.

Pettersvold, M., & Østrem, S. (2012). *Mestrer – mestrer ikke: Jakten på det normale barnet* [Master – Do not Master: The Hunt for the Normal Child]. Oslo: Res Publica.

Pillet-Shore, D. (2003). Doing 'okay': On the multiple metrics of an assessment. *Research on Language & Social Interaction, 36*(3), 285–319.

Plantin, L., & Danebeck, K. (2009). Parenthood, information and support on the internet: A literature review of research on parents and professionals online. *BMC Family Practice, 34*(10), 10–34.

Popham, W. J. (2008). *Transformative Assessment*. Alexandria, VA: Association for Supervision and Curriculum Development (ASCD).

Popkewitz, T. S. (2003). Governing the child and pedagogicalization of the parent. In M. N. Block, K. Holmlund, I. Moqvist, & T. S. Popkewitz. (Eds.), *Governing Children, Families and Education: Restructuring the Welfare State* (pp. 35–61). New York: Palgrave.

Popkewitz, T. S. (2008). *Cosmopolitanism and the Age of School Reform: Science, Education, and Making Society by Making the Child*. New York: Routledge.

Powell, D. R., & Diamond, K. E. (1995) Approaches to parent–teacher relationships in the US: Early childhood programs during the twentieth century. *Journal of Education, 177*(3), 71–94.

Power, M. (1997). *The Audit Society: Rituals of Verifications*. Oxford: Oxford University Press.

Prasad, M. (2006). *The Politics of Free Markets: The Rise of Neoliberal Economic Policies in Britain, France, Germany, and the United States*. Chicago: University of Chicago Press.

Prior, L. (2003). *Using documents in social research*. London: Sage.

Prior, L. (2008). Repositioning documents in social research. *Sociology, 42*(5), 821–36.

Pugh, A. J. (2009). *Longing and Belonging: Parents, Children, and Consumer Culture*. California: University of California Press.

Putnam, L. L., & Cooren, F. S. (2004). Alternative perspectives on the role of text and agency in constituting organizations. *Organization, 11*(3), 323–33.

Qvortrup, J. (2012). Users and interested parties: A concluding essay on children's institutionalization. In A. T. Kjørholt, & J. Qvortrup (Eds.), *The Modern Child and the Flexible Labour Market. Early Childhood Education and Care* (pp. 243–61). Basingstoke: Palgrave Macmillan.

Ravn, B. (2005). An ambiguous relationship: Challenges and contradictions in the field of family–school community partnership: Questioning the discourse of partnership. In R.-A. Martinnez-Gonzales, et al. *Family–School Community Partnerships Merging into Social Development* (pp. 453–47). Oveido, Spain: GrupoSM.

Rhedding-Jones (1996). Positionings poststructural: Some Australian research in education. *Nordisk Pedagogik, 16*(1): 2–14.

Rinaldi, C. (2005). Documentation and assessment: What is the relationship? In A. Clark, A. T. Kjørholt, & P. Moss (Eds.), *Beyond Listening: Children's Perspectives on Early Childhood Services* (pp. 17–28). Bristol: The Policy Press.

Robinson, K. H., & Díaz, C. J. (2006). *Diversity and Difference in Early Childhood Education: Issues for Theory and Practice*. Berkshire: Open University Press.

Rodriguez, M. d. C., Pena, J.V., Fernandez, C. M., & Vinuela, M. P. (2006). Gender discourse about an ethic of care: Nursery schoolteachers' perspectives. *Gender and Education, 18*(2), 183–97.

Rogoff, B. (2003). *The Cultural Nature of Child Development*. New York: Oxford University Press.

Rose, N. (1996a). *Inventing Our-Selves: Psychology, Power, and Personhood*. Cambridge: Cambridge University Press.

Rose, N. (1996b). Governing 'advanced' liberal democracies. In A. Barry, T. Osborne, & N. Rose (Eds.), *Foucault and Political Reason: Liberalism, Neo-Liberalism and Rationalities of Government* (pp. 37–63). Chicago: University of Chicago Press.

Rose, N. (1999a). *Governing the Soul: The Shaping of the Private Self*. London: Free Association Press.

Rose, N. (1999b). *Powers of Freedom: Reframing Political Thought*. Cambridge: Cambridge University Press.

Rose, N., O'Malley, P., & Valverde, M. (2006). Governmentality. *Annual Review of Law and Social Science, 2*, 83–104.

Rose, N., & Miller, P. (2008). *Governing the Present: Administering Economic, Social and Personal Life*. Cambridge: Polity.

Säljö, R., & Hjörne, E. (2009). *Att platsa i en skola för alla* [To Qualify in a School for All]. Stockholm: Norstedts akademiska förlag.

Sammons, P., Elliot, K., Sylva, K., Melhuish, E., Siraj-Blatchford, I., & Taggart, B. (2004). The impact of pre-school on young children's cognitive attainments at entry to reception. *British Educational Research Journal, 30*(5), 691–712.

Sandberg, A., & Vourinen, T. (2007). *Hem och förskola: Samverkan i förändring* [Home and Preschool: Collaboration in Change]. Stockholm: Liber.

Satka, M., & Harrikari, T. (2008). The present Finnish formation of child welfare and history. *British Journal of Social Work, 38*, 645–661.

Schwandt, T. A. (2012). Quality, standards and accountability: An uneasy alliance. *Education Inquiry, 3*(2), 217–24.

Segerholm, C. (2012). The quality turn: Political and methodological challenges in contemporary educational evaluation and assessment. *Education Inquiry, 3*(2), 115–22.

Sheridan, S. (2009). Dimensions of pedagogical quality in preschool. *International Journal of Early Years Education, 15*(2), 197–217.

Sheridan, S., Pramling Samuelsson, I., & Johansson, E. (2009). *Barns tidiga lärande: En tvärsnittsstudie av förskolan som miljö för barns lärande* [Children's Early Learning: A Cross-Sectional Study of Preschool as an Environment for Children's Learning]. Göteborg, Sweden: Acta Universitatis Gothoburgensis.

Silverman, D. (2006). *Interpreting Qualitative Data: Methods for Analyzing Talk, Text and Interaction*. Los Angeles, CA: Sage.

Silverman, D., Baker, C., & Keogh, J. (1998). The case of the silent child: Advice-giving and advice reception in parent–teacher interviews. In I. Hutchby, & J. Moran-Ellis (Eds.), *Children and Social Competence* (pp. 220–40). London: Falmer Press.

Simonsson, M., & Markström, A.-M. (2013). Utvecklingssamtal som uppgift och verktyg i förskolärares professionssträvanden i interaktion med föräldrar [Developmental talks as a

task and tool in preschool teacher's strives for professionality in interaction with parents].
Nordisk Barnehageforskning, 6(12), 1–18.

Skolverket [National Agency for Education] (2008a). *Tio år efter förskolereformen: Nationell utvärdering av förskolan* [Ten Years After the Pre-School Reform: National Evaluation of Preschool]. Stockholm: Fritzes.

Skolverket [National Agency for Education] (2008b). *Allmänna råd och kommentarer: Den individuella utvecklingsplanen med skriftliga omdömen* [Guidelines and Comments: The Individual Development Plan With Written Reviews]. Stockholm: Fritzes.

Skolverket [National Agency for Education] (2010). *Läroplan för förskolan: Reviderad 2010* [Curriculum for the Preschool: Revised 2010]. Retrieved 5 September 2012 from http://www.skolverket.se/publikationer?id=2704.

Skolverket [National Agency for Education] (2012). *Uppföljning, utvärdering och utveckling i förskolan – Pedagogisk dokumentation* [Monitoring, Evaluation and Development in Preschool – Pedagogical Documentation]. Stockholm: Fritzes.

Sparkes, A. C., & Smith, B. (2007). Narrative constructionist inquiry. In J. A. Holstein, & J. F. Gubrium (Eds.), *Handbook of Constructionist Research* (pp. 295–314). New York: Guildford Press.

Spyrou, S. (2011). The limits of children's voices: From authenticity to critical, reflexive representation. *Childhood, 18*(2), 151–65.

Stakes (2004). *National Curriculum Guidelines on Early Childhood and Care in Finland.* Helsinki: Stakes. Retrieved 24 June 2012 from http://www.thl.fi/thl-client/pdfs/267671cb-0ec0-4039-b97b-7ac6ce6b9c10.

Star, S. L., & Griesemer, J. R. (1989). Institutional ecology, 'translations' and boundary objects: Amateurs and professionals in Berkeley's Museum of Vertebrate Zoology, 1907–39. *Social Studies of Science, 19*(4), 387–420.

Steyerl, H. (2003). *Documentarism as Politics of Truth.* Retrieved 19 September 2010 from eipcp.net/transversal/1003/steyerl2/en.

Strandell, H. (2011). Policies of early childhood education and care: Partnership and individualisation. In A. T. Kjørholt, & J. Qvortrup (Eds.), *The Modern Child and the Flexible Labour Market: Child Care Policies and Practices at a Crossroad?* (pp. 222–40). Basingstoke: Palgrave Macmillan.

Sulkunen, P. (2007). Re-inventing the social contract. *Acta Sociologica, 50*(3), 325–33.

Sulkunen, P. (2009). *The Saturated Society: Governing Risk and Lifestyles in Consumer Culture.* London: Sage.

Sundblad, B. (2006). *RUS: Relationsutvecklingsschema* [RUS: Relational Development Schedule]. Retrieved 12 June 2013 from http://www.bibo.se/pdf/rus/RUS_manual%20. pdf.

Swedish Education Act (2010) SFS 2010:800. *Skollag.*

Symeou, L. (2007). Cultural capital and family involvement in children's education: Tales from two primary schools in Cyprus. *British Journal of Sociology of Education, 28*(4), 473–87.

Taggart, Brenda (2004). Early years education and care: Three agendas. *British Educational Research Journal, 30*(5), 619–22.

Tannen, D. (1993). *Framing in Discourse.* New York: Oxford University Press.

Taras, M. (2009). Summative assessment: The missing link for formative assessment. *Journal of Further and Higher Education, 33*(1), 57–69.

Tayler, C. (2006). Challenging partnerships in Australian early childhood education. *Early Years: Journal of International Research & Development, 26*(3), 249–65.

Thomas, G., & Pring, R. (Eds.) (2004). *Evidence-Based Practice in Education.* Buckingham: Open University Press.

Trondman, M. (2011). Snälla fröknar – om barns perspektiv och barnperspektiv [Nice teachers – about children's perspectives and a child perspective]. In I. Tallberg Broman (Ed.), *Skola och barndom: Normering, demokratisering, individualisering* [School and Childhood: Normalization, Democratization, Individualization] (pp. 67–80). Malmö: Gleerups förlag.

Trondman, M., Lund, A., & Mast, J. L. (Eds.) (2011). *Jeffrey C. Alexander: Kulturell sociologi – Program, teori och praktik* [Jeffrey C. Alexander: Cultural Sociology – Program Theory and Practice]. Göteborg: Daidalos.

Turmel, A. (2008). *A Historical Sociology of Childhood. Developmental Thinking, Categorization and Graphic Visualization.* Cambridge: Cambridge University Press.

Tveit, A. D. (2007). Conditional aspects of school–home conversations. *International Journal about Parents in Education, 1,* 200–9.

Uljens, M. (Ed.) (1997). *Didaktik – teori, reflektion och praktik* [Didaktik – Theory, Reflection and Practice]. Lund: Studentlitteratur.

Uljens, M. (2006). *Vad är bildning?* [What is Formation?] Retrieved 22 February 2013 from http://www.vasa.abo.fi/users/muljens/pdf/Vad_ar_bildning.pdf.

Välimäki, A.-L., & Rauhala, P.-L. (2000). Lasten päivähoidon taipuminen yhteiskunnallisiin murroksiin Suomessa [Children's day care yields to societal changes in Finland]. *Yhteiskuntapolitiikka, 65*(5), 387–405.

Vallberg-Roth, A.-C. (2006). Early childhood curricula in Sweden: From the 1850s to the present. *International Journal of Early Childhood, 38*(1), 77–98.

Vallberg-Roth, A.-C. (2009). Styrning genom bedömning av barn [Steering through assessment of children]. *EDUCARE, 2–3,* 195–219.

Vallberg-Roth, A.-C. (2010). Att stödja och styra barns lärande – tidig bedömning och dokumentation [To support and steer children's learning – early assessment and documentation]. In Skolverket [National Agency for Education] *Perspektiv på barndom och barns lärande i förskola och grundskolans tidigare år: En kunskapsöversikt* [Perspectives on Childhood and Children's Learning in Preschool and Early School Years: A Knowledge Review] (pp. 176–234). Skolverket: Fritzes.

Vallberg-Roth, A.-C. (2011a). 'Gör alltid sitt bästa' 'Duktig! Kan ibland vara lite stökig' – Om bedömning och dokumentation av barn ['Always do their best' 'Talented! Can sometimes be a little messy' – about assessment and documentation of children]. In I. Tallberg-Broman (Ed.) *Skola och barndom: Normering, demokratisering, individualisering* [School and Childhood: Normalization, Democratization, Individualization] (pp. 117–41). Malmö: Gleerups förlag

Vallberg-Roth, A.-C. (2011b). *De yngre barnens läroplanshistoria – didaktik, dokumentation och bedömning i förskola* [The Younger Children's Curriculum History – Didaktik, Documentation and Assessment in Preschool] (2nd ed.). Lund: Studentlitteratur.

Vallberg-Roth, A.-C. (2012a). Parenthood in intensified documentation and assessment practice – with the focus on the home–school relation in Sweden. *International Journal about Parents in Education, 6*(1), 41–54.

Vallberg-Roth, A.-C. (2012b). Different forms of assessment and documentation in Swedish preschools. *Nordic Early Childhood Education Research, 5*(23), 1–18.

Vallberg-Roth, A.-C. (2013a). *Nordisk komparativ analys av riktlinjer för kvalitet och innehåll i förskolorna* [Nordic Comparative Analysis of Guidelines for Quality and Content in ECE]. Oslo: Kunskapsdepartementet (in progress).

Vallberg-Roth, A.-C. (2013b). Styrning genom dokumentation och bedömning – dokumentalitet [Steering through documentation and assessment – Documentality]. In J. Qvarsebo, & J. Balldin (Eds.), *Utbildning, Samtid, Styrning* [Education, Contemporaries, Governance]. Lund: Studentlitteratur (in press).

Vallberg-Roth, A.-C., & Månsson A. (2006). Individuella utvecklingsplaner som fenomen i tiden, samhället och skolan [Individual development plans as a phenomenon of the times, of society and of school]. *Utbildning & Demokrati, 15*(3), 31–60.

Vallberg-Roth, A.-C., & Månsson, A. (2008). Individuella utvecklingsplaner som uttryck för reglerad barndom: Likriktning med variation [Individual development plans as expressions of regulated childhood: Equivalence with variation]. *Pedagogisk forskning i Sverige, 13*(2), 81–102.

Vallberg-Roth, A.-C., & Månsson A. (2009). Regulated childhood: Equivalence with variation. *Early Years, 2,* 1–14.

Vallberg-Roth, A.-C., & Månsson, A. (2011). Individual development plans in a critical didactic perspective: Focusing on Montessori- and Reggio Emilia-profiled preschools in Sweden. *Journal of Early Childhood Research, 9*(3), 251–65.

Vandenbroeck, M., Boonaert, T., van Der Mespel, S., & de Brabaundere, K. (2009). Dialogical spaces to reconceptualize parent support in the social investment state. *Contemporary Issues in Early Childhood, 10*(1), 66–77.

Vandenbroeck, M., & Bouverne-De Bie, M. (2006). Children's agency and educational norms: A tensed negotiation. *Childhood, 13*(1), 127–43.

Vandenbroeck, M., Coussée, F., & Bradt, L. (2010). The social and political construction of early childhood education. *British Journal of Educational Studies, 58*(2), 139–53.

Vandenbroeck, M., Roets, G., & Snoeck, A. (2009). Immigrant mothers crossing borders: Nomadic identities and multiple belongings in early childhood education. *European Early Childhood Education Research Journal, 17*(2), 203–16.

Vásquez, C. (2009). Examining the role of face work in a workplace complaint narrative. *Narrative Inquiry, 19*(2), 259–79.

Vincent, C. (1996). *Parents and Teacher: Power and Participation.* London: Falmer Press.

Vincent, C., & Martin, J. (2000). School-based parent's groups: A politics of voice and representation? *Journal of Education Policy, 15*(5) 459–80.

Vincent, C., & Tomlinson, S. (1997). Home–school relationships: 'The swarming of disciplinary mechanisms'. *British Educational Research Journal, 23*(3) 361–67.

Vyverman, Veerle, & Vettenburg, Nicole (2009). Parent participation at school: A research study on the perspectives of children. *Childhood, 16*(1), 105–23.

Wagner, Å., & Kari, H. (2004). Ordproduktion [Word production]. In U. Espenakk, et al. (Eds.), *TRAS Tidig registrering av språkutveckling: En handbok om språkutveckling hos barn* [TRAS Early Registration of Language Development: A Handbook on Language Development Among Children] (pp. 104–10). Herning: SPF-utbildning.com.

Wagner, J. T. (2006). An outsider's perspective. Childhoods and early education in the Nordic countries. In J. Einarsdottir, & J. T. Wagner (Eds.), *Nordic Childhoods and Early Education: Philosophy, Research, Policy, and Practice in Denmark, Finland, Iceland, Norway, and Sweden* (pp. 289–306). Greenwich, CT: Information Age.

Walkerdine, V. (1990). *Schoolgirl Fictions.* New York: Verso.

Warming, Hanne (2005). Participant observation: A way to learn about children's perspectives. In A. Clark, A. T. Kjørholt, & P. Moss (Eds.), *Beyond Listening. Children's Perspectives on Early Childhood Services* (pp. 51–70). Bristol: Policy Press.

Woodhead, M. (2005). Early childhood development: A question of rights. *Journal of Early childhood, 37*(3), 79–98.

INDEX

CPSIA information can be obtained
at www.ICGtesting.com
Printed in the USA
LVOW10s0715140817

544928LV00010B/277/P